LiTTLE GUiDES

Dangerous Animals

LiTTLE GUiDES

Dangerous
Animals

Consultant Editor
Dr George McKay

FOG CITY PRESS

Published by Fog City Press
814 Montgomery Street
San Francisco, CA 94133 USA

Copyright © 2006 Weldon Owen Inc.
First printed 2006

Chief Executive Officer: John Owen
President: Terry Newell
Publisher: Sheena Coupe
Creative Director: Sue Burk
Project Management: Limelight Press Pty Ltd
Project Editor: Scott Forbes
Series Design: Nika Markovtzev
Project Designer: Avril Makula
Editorial Coordinator: Helen Flint
Production Director: Chris Hemesath
Production Coordinator: Charles Mathews
Sales Manager: Emily Bartle
Vice President International Sales: Stuart Laurence
Administrator International Sales: Kristine Ravn

ISBN 13: 978-1-74089-544-6

Color reproduction by SC (Sang Choy) International Pte Ltd
Printed by SNP Leefung Printers Ltd
Printed in China

A Weldon Owen Production
Produced using arkiva retrieval technology
For further information, contact arkiva@weldonowen.com.au

Contents

A Dangerous World

Danger lurks in every corner of the animal kingdom. A tiger can kill with one bite. A charging rhino can gore with its horn. A nip from a spider can kill in minutes. Even a tiny fly can pass on a deadly disease. But most animals are much more dangerous to each other than to humans. They use their weapons mainly to hunt, fight, or scare off other creatures. Only occasionally do they hurt people, and usually only to defend themselves.

WELL ARMED

Animals have developed an amazing array of weapons. They range from sharp teeth, horns, and claws to poisonous spines and stings.

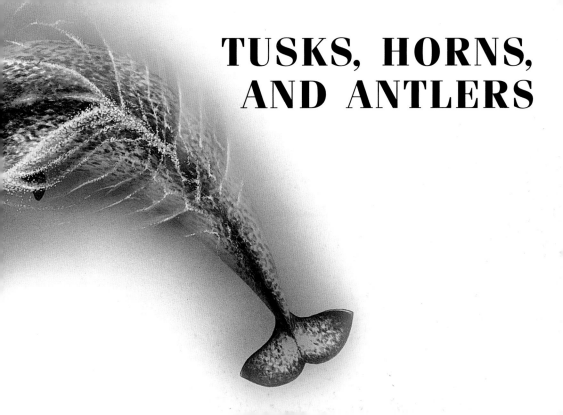

TUSKS, HORNS, AND ANTLERS

Giants of the Land

The biggest land animals on Earth are elephants. They can stand 13 feet (4 m) tall and reach a length of almost 25 feet (7.5 m), and they can weigh up to 7 tons (6.3 tonnes)—as much as 200 10-year-old children! That makes them dangerous to anything that gets in their way, especially when they are running. Aside from its weight, an elephant's main weapon is its tusks, which it can use to cut or stab rivals or predators.

FILLING UP
Elephants spend up to 21 hours a day looking for and eating food. In just one day, they can munch their way through as much as 330 pounds (150 kg) of leaves, bark, fruits, and grass, and guzzle 40 gallons (160 liters) of water.

Growing Fast

Female elephants are pregnant for up to two years, which is the longest pregnancy of any mammal. Usually, they have just one calf at a time and continue to feed it for the first 12 to 18 months of its life. By the time an elephant is six years old, it weighs about 1 ton (1 tonne)—as much as a small car. It continues to increase rapidly in size until about age 15. After that, it grows more slowly, but it may live for up to 70 years.

40 years

15 years

10 years

6 years

3 years

1 year

6 months

HEIGHT CHART
This illustration shows how an elephant develops over its lifetime. Tusks usually begin to grow between two and three years of age.

Big Ears

There are two kinds of elephants: the African elephant and the Asian elephant. African elephants are taller and heavier than Asian elephants and have much bigger ears. They live in deserts and forests, but mainly on grasslands called savannas. The elephants that live in forests are usually slightly smaller than other African elephants.

Where elephants live in Africa

FAMILY DIFFERENCES

Elephants can walk short distances within hours of their birth. Within two days they can keep up with the herd. All adult African elephants have tusks, though the male's are larger.

Beasts of Burden

Asian elephants are smaller and lighter than African elephants and have much smaller ears. They live mainly in the forests and grasslands of southern Asia. People in these regions often train elephants to do jobs such as moving logs and carrying goods and passengers.

Asian elephants have more rounded heads and sloping backs than African elephants. Females never have tusks.

Where elephants live in Asia

IN THE PINK
Male Asian elephants are larger than females and can reach a height of 10 feet (3 m). Asian elephants often have pink patches on their faces.

Head to Head

An elephant uses its trunk to smell and breathe. But it also uses it to move objects, lift food to its mouth, spray itself with water, and make sounds and signals. A trunk is strong enough to pull a tree out of the ground, but dainty enough to pick up a coin. Tusks are not horns, but very large teeth. They grow longer as an elephant gets older. Elephants use their tusks not only as a weapon, but also to scrape bark off trees and to dig for water.

DEADLY DUEL
An elephant also uses its trunk for fighting. Battles between rival males can be violent, occasionally leading to the death of one competitor.

The Asian elephant has smaller ears and shorter tusks.

ASIAN TRUNK

The Asian elephant has only one "finger" at the end of its trunk.

Nerve endings at top of tusk

INSIDE THE TRUNK

An elephant's trunk has no bones, but is made up of about 150,000 bands of muscle. Like our teeth, tusks contain nerve endings. That means elephants can feel pressure through their tusks.

21

The Bare Bones

Over thousands of years, elephants have developed features that support their enormous weight. Their legs, which look like wide tree trunks, contain massive, dense bones that help them stay on their feet for long periods. The bones of the upper body are lighter and more slender, but still very strong.

FRONT VIEW OF FOOT

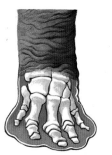

An elephant's toes are protected by a tough, hooflike covering of skin.

SIDE VIEW OF FOOT

Thick pads behind an elephant's toes help support its weight.

BUILT FOR STRENGTH
An elephant's head can weigh 660 pounds (300 kg), so the bones and muscles that hold it up have to be very strong. The skull contains air pockets that help reduce its weight.

DID YOU KNOW?

An elephant's heels are raised off the ground—so elephants walk on tiptoes!

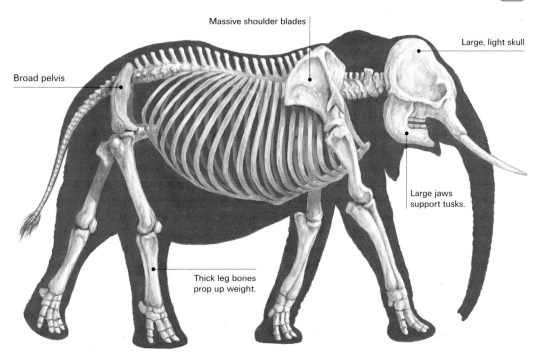

Massive shoulder blades

Large, light skull

Broad pelvis

Large jaws
support tusks.

Thick leg bones
prop up weight.

Family Life

Female elephants and their young live in large family groups called herds, which can sometimes include hundreds of elephants. When they are about 13 years old, male elephants leave the herd to live alone or with other males. They return to visit the herd only during the mating season. At that time, the males fight each other using their trunk and tusks to decide who will mate with the females. Female elephants use their tusks to keep predators away from their young.

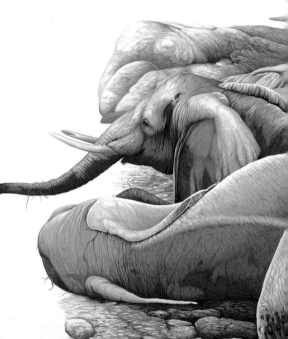

COOLING OFF
When it is hot, elephants cool off in rivers and pools. They use their trunks to suck up water and spray themselves. They also cover themselves in mud, which protects them from the sun and insects.

24

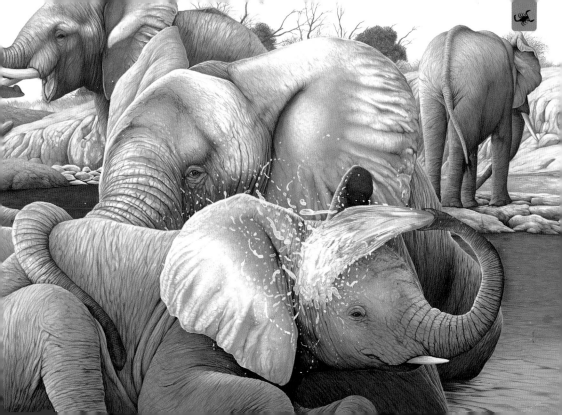

Open Wide

Male hippopotamuses often fight fiercely over food, territory, and females. They do this by opening their jaws wide, locking their teeth together, and pushing against each other. Fights can last for up to an hour and a half. All hippos will chase off predators and can be dangerous to humans who enter their territory.

SUN SMART
Hippos spend most of the day resting in water to stay cool and prevent sunburn. For extra protection, their skin produces a red substance, which acts like sunscreen.

TWIN PRONGS
A hippo can open its mouth very wide. Its large hornlike teeth are its most dangerous weapon.

Little and Large

There are two types of hippos and both live only in Africa. The hippopotamus can grow to 14 feet (4.2 m) long and reach a height of 5 feet (1.5 m) and a weight of 2¼ tons (2 tonnes). The pygmy hippopotamus, as its name suggests, is much smaller— roughly half the length and height and just one-seventh of the weight of its bulkier relative. Hippopotamuses often gather in large groups in lakes and rivers. Pygmy hippos are shy and tend to wander alone and stay hidden in swamps and forests.

Where hippos live in Africa

Where pygmy hippos live in Africa

IN THE SWIM
They may seem clumsy, but hippos are extremely good swimmers. They use their back legs to push themselves through the water. They close their nostrils and ears, staying underwater for up to 5 minutes at a time.

RARE BREED
Pygmy hippos have always been rare, and today only a few thousand survive in the wild. They are still hunted for their meat and teeth.

Scouring the Seas

The walrus is the largest member of a group of meat-eating marine mammals called the pinnipeds, which also includes seals and sea lions. Walruses can grow to 11½ feet (3.5 m) long and 3,640 pounds (1,650 kg) in weight. All have large, sharp tusks. Walruses eat mainly shellfish, especially clams, and some fish, but when food is scarce they may also eat baby seals.

Walruses live in shallow Arctic seas.

EXPERT SWIMMER
Although it is heavy, the walrus is a very good swimmer. On land, it is clumsy, but can move quite quickly on its four broad flippers.

BY A WHISKER
The walrus uses the long, sensitive whiskers on the side of its face to find worms, crabs, shrimps, and mussels buried in sand on the seafloor.

31

Tusk, Tusk

The tusks of the walrus are the most obvious difference between it and its relatives, the seals and sea lions. As with elephant tusks, walrus tusks are actually long teeth that grow from sockets set deep in the jaw. Walruses use their tusks to dig up food, pull themselves onto ice floes, battle rivals, and fight off predators, which sometimes include humans.

PACKING THEM IN
Walruses spend much of their time in large colonies of up to 3,000 animals. The largest animals with the longest tusks usually dominate the others.

CHECK THESE OUT
By displaying his tusks prominently, a male walrus can defeat a smaller rival without landing a single blow. Seeing large tusks, a weaker male will quickly realize he would be foolish to fight.

DID YOU KNOW?

A male walrus's tusks can reach a length of more than 3 feet (1 m).

Jousting Whales

The most spectacular tusk in the animal world belongs to the narwhal, a species of whale that lives in the icy waters of the Arctic Ocean. The narwhal has just two teeth, on its upper jaw. In the male, the left tooth grows out through the top lip, forming a long, spiraling tusk with a sharp point, which can measure 10 feet (3 m) in length.

DUEL IN THE DEEP
Rival male narwhals use their tusks like swords to fight each other. Young narwhals usually just play, but older males often draw blood.

On the Rampage

You would not want to get in the way of a charging rhino! It can weigh up to 4 tons (3.6 tonnes)—more than a small truck—move at 30 miles an hour (45 km/h), and usually has at least one large and very sharp horn. Rhinoceroses are generally aggressive and will charge whenever they feel threatened. Males and females also fight rivals regularly—often to the death.

SKIN CARE
A rhino's thick gray skin has deep folds that make it look like armor. The rhino protects its skin from heat and insects by regularly covering it with mud.

QUICK TO REACT
The black rhinoceros is particularly bad tempered and will charge anything unfamiliar, including humans and vehicles. It uses its two sharp horns to gore and toss predators such as these spotted hyenas.

Rhino Routines

Rhinos live in Africa, India, and Southeast Asia, mainly in grasslands, marshes, and forests. They are plant-eaters and feed on grass, leaves, and saplings. Most rhinos spend their time alone in their own territory. They mark this territory by leaving piles of their dung and urine along its boundaries. Though they do not see well, rhinos have a good sense of smell, as well as excellent hearing. When they are not feeding, rhinos sleep, or cool off in mud or water.

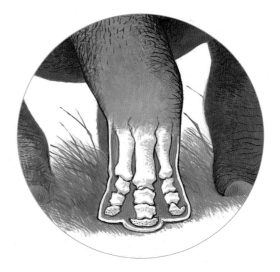

A SOLID FOOTING
Rhinos are on their feet for much of the day, so they need strong, muscular legs to support their massive body. Each leg stands on a broad foot with three wide toes.

MOWING THE LAWN

The broad, strong lips of the white rhino are ideally suited to chomping grass. African rhinos are often accompanied by birds called oxpeckers, which eat the insects they stir up.

LIP SERVICE

Other rhinos have a long, pointed upper lip that they can use to pull branches down to their mouth. The lip can be tucked away when the rhino is eating short grasses.

Hunted for Their Horns

There are five kinds of rhinos: the white rhinoceros and the black rhinoceros, which live in Africa; and the Indian, Javan, and Sumatran rhinos, which are found in Asia. Demand for rhino horns, for use in traditional medicine and for carving, has led to all five being hunted. Today fewer than 15,000 rhinos survive in Africa and no more than 3,000 in Asia.

MAP KEY

■ Former range

■ Current range

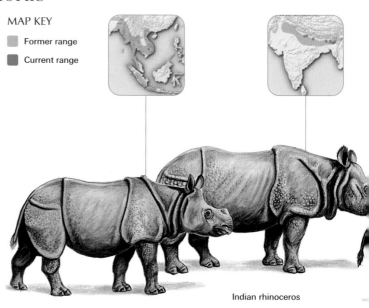

Indian rhinoceros

Javan rhinoceros

SPOT THE DIFFERENCES
Both African rhinoceroses have two horns. Of the Asian rhinos, only the Sumatran has two; the others just one.

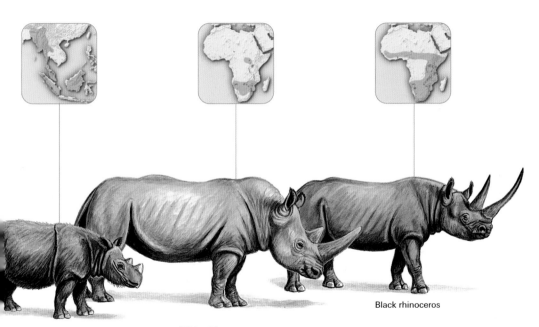

Sumatran rhinoceros

White rhinoceros

Black rhinoceros

41

Mother and Child

Rhinos can have only one baby every two to four years so it is important that they take great care of each one. Mothers nurse their calf for at least a year and usually stay with it until the next calf is born. If the mother senses any threat to her young, she may charge. If she is with other rhinos, the adults may form a protective ring around the young.

A CLOSE WATCH
A young rhino always stays close to its mother, normally walking by her side, as shown here, or just a few steps ahead of her.

TEAMWORK
If several white rhinos are attacked in a group, they sometimes form a circle with their horns facing outward to keep predators away.

Branching Out

Antlers grow on moose, caribou, and almost all male deer. They range in size from small spikes to large treelike shapes, known as racks. Male animals with antlers use them to fight other males. They also display them to females to show that they are strong and healthy and will therefore be a good mate.

WHEN PUSH COMES TO SHOVE
Male caribou use their antlers in fights that decide who will mate with the females of the herd. They lock their antlers together, then push as hard as they can. The caribou that gives way and runs off is the loser.

44

New for Old

An animal with tusks or horns will usually keep them for life. But deer, moose, and caribou shed their antlers and grow a new set once a year. Each year, the antlers grow a little bigger, so the size of an animal's antlers tells you how old it is.

SKIN AND BONE

Antlers are bones. Horns are made of keratin (a hard skin also found in our fingernails), or keratin-covered bone.

Bone ▢

Bone that is shed ▢

Keratin ▢

Bongo

White-tailed deer

Black rhinoceros

SPRING

Antlers usually begin to grow in late spring. At first, they are covered in soft skin called velvet.

SUMMER

By late summer, the antlers have reached their full size and grown hard. The velvet begins to dry out.

AUTUMN

The animal rubs the velvet off on bushes and trees. It is now ready to take part in contests and displays.

WINTER

When the mating season is over, the two antlers fall off, usually within days of each other.

The Magnificent Moose

The male moose is not only the largest of all deer, but has the most magnificent set of antlers of any animal. Like other male deer, the male moose uses his antlers for contests and displays. Moose can be irritable and may charge or kick humans and other animals that get in their way or too close to their young.

CREATURES OF THE SWAMPS
Moose live in northern North America, Europe, and Asia. In Europe they are called elk. They like swampy areas, where they often stand in water, munching plants.

DID YOU KNOW?

Moose are good swimmers and will often jump into water to escape predators.

GROWING A RACK

In its first year, a moose grows antlers like small spikes.

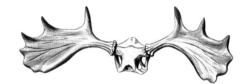

By its fourth year, the moose has a wide rack with several branches.

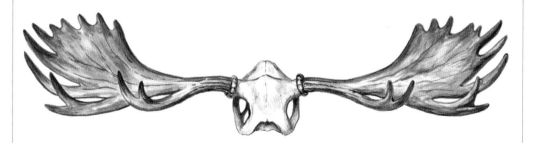

A mature moose has a rack with numerous branches and points, which can be up to 6½ feet (2 m) wide.

Locking Horns

Male and female members of the cattle family, including cows, antelopes, sheep, and goats, all have horns. Usually, the horns consist of bone covered with hard skin called keratin. Horns show an animal's age and status, and are used in territorial or mating contests. Most of these animals prefer to run away from predators, but they will sometimes charge them.

Sheep approach each other.

Exchange kicks.

BATTLE OF THE BIGHORNS
Mating contests between male bighorn sheep can last 24 hours. They usually include the stages shown here.

Smash horns together.

DIFFERENT DESIGNS
Many antelopes, like this eland, have spiraling horns. The shape helps lock the horns together during contests.

Pull away from each other.

Rear onto hind legs.

Display horns.

Pause to feed.

TEETH AND CLAWS: CREATURES OF THE LAND

King of the Dinosaurs

Sharp teeth and claws are essential tools for any meat-eating creatures. Few predators have ever been as large and powerful as the meat-eating dinosaurs that roamed Earth during the Mesozoic era, between 245 and 65 million years ago. The king of these dinosaurs was *Tyrannosaurus*. It was larger and heavier than an African elephant and was equipped with teeth and claws that could kill almost any other creature.

HANDY CLAWS

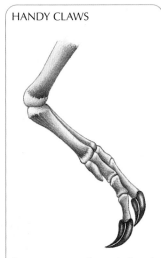

Tyrannosaurus ran fast on its broad back legs. Its small hands, seen here, had two large, sharp claws that it used to hook and hold prey.

MEGA BITES

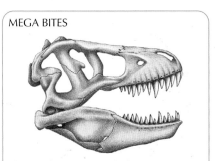

The jaw of *Tyrannosaurus* had an extra joint so that it could take especially large bites.

COMING AT YOU!
A charging *Tyrannosaurus* would have been a terrifying sight! It was taller than a double-decker bus and its huge mouth contained more than 50 teeth.

Team Players

Many smaller meat-eating dinosaurs were almost as fierce as *Tyrannosaurus*. *Velociraptor* and *Deinonychus*, for example, had strong jaws and razor-sharp claws. They hunted in packs and could outrun most other creatures. Once they caught up with their prey, they would encircle it and take turns to distract it while others attacked from behind, slashing with their claws. Eventually, the prey would tire, fall to the ground, and be devoured by the pack.

LETHAL WEAPON

Deinonychus had one long claw on each foot, which it could swivel up and down to cut deep wounds in prey. Its name, *Deinonychus*, means "terrible claw."

BUILT TO KILL

A combination of strong bones, powerful leg and jaw muscles, and the camouflage of a feathery covering made *Deinonychus* a fearful predator.

57

The Fast Robber

The name *Velociraptor* means "fast robber," and its speed certainly gave this meat-eater a great advantage over many of the slower animals it hunted—mainly small plant-eaters. It used its long tail to help it balance and its sharp claws to rip and tear at flesh. Like *Deinonychus*, *Velociraptor* had one very large claw on each foot. Fossils suggest it used these claws to kill its prey.

PINT-SIZED PREDATOR
Velociraptor was smaller than *Deinonychus*, standing 6 feet (1.8 m) tall and weighing 100 pounds (45 kg), roughly as much as a 13-year-old child.

CLAW CARE

Velociraptor held its large claws off the ground to keep them sharp.

FEATHERED FOSSILS

Fossils discovered recently indicate that *Velociraptor* and *Deinonychus* may have had feathers. So *Velociraptor* could have looked something like this.

Eating Habits

BITE AND PULL

Tyrannosaurus's teeth were 6 inches (15 cm) long, but not sharp enough to cut flesh. Instead, *Tyrannosaurus* ripped off big bits of flesh and swallowed them whole.

TACKLING FISH

Baryonyx hooked fish out of streams with a long, sharp, curved claw on its hand. The teeth of *Baryonyx* were shaped like those of today's fish-eating crocodiles.

SNAP AND SWALLOW

Some meat-eaters didn't have teeth. *Gallimimus* probably used its narrow beak to snap up insects, eggs, small animals, and other foods it could devour in one gulp.

QUICK HANDS

Compsognathus used its small, quick, nimble hands to grab prey such as lizards. It would hold them tight, bite off large pieces, and swallow them almost whole.

Killer Cats

There are 36 kinds of wild cats. All are expert hunters and eat mostly meat. Usually, they sneak up on other animals, then pounce. Cats have muscular bodies, excellent sight and hearing, pointed claws for holding prey, and razor-sharp teeth for killing and devouring. Occasionally, large cats kill people, but usually only when they are sick, hurt, or short of food.

DINNER RUSH
A lion may hunt alone or with other lions. It stalks animals silently, often for a long time. Then it dashes forward, grabs its prey with its huge claws, and kills it with a bite to the neck that crushes its windpipe.

THE BIG GUYS
Cats are all much the same shape, but they come in all sorts of sizes. Lions, tigers, jaguars, and leopards are known as "the big cats." Although all cats purr, only the big cats can roar.

Pride of the Plains

Lions live on the African plains and have few rivals there. They can even kill creatures much larger than themselves. Unlike most other cats, which are solitary, lions live in groups called prides. These include up to 20 females (which are called lionesses), their cubs, and a couple of dominant males. Until they win control of a pride, males live alone or with other males.

IN THE LION'S MOUTH

A lioness often uses her mouth to carry small cubs around.

BIG BOYS

Adult male lions have a golden or dark brown mane. They can be up to 7½ feet (2.3 m) long and are about one and half times the size of females.

Where lions live in Africa and India

DID YOU KNOW?

Lionesses do most of the hunting, though they usually let dominant males eat first.

Stand Off

Tigers are the biggest of big cats, measuring up to 12 feet (3.6 m) long—imagine two tall people lying end to end and you get some idea of their length! In the grasslands and forests of Asia, where tigers live, their stripes provide camouflage. That means they can sneak up undetected, then surprise their prey. Like other cats, tigers use sounds and visual signals to warn rivals not to attack or to show that they are ready for a fight.

DID YOU KNOW?

To survive, a tiger needs to kill and eat a large animal every three to five days.

BACK OFF!

The margay, an Asian cat, shows it will fight by opening its eyes wide.

HERE I COME!

Lowered ears and bared teeth warn that the margay is ready to attack.

MAKING A CHALLENGE

Tigers live alone and mark out their territory with their scent. When rival tigers meet, they show that they are ready to fight by rotating their ears so that the white spots on the back of their ears face forward.

The High Life

Cats spend most of their time on the ground, but many can swim well and most are good climbers. Their sharp claws help them grab hold of tree trunks and other rough surfaces. Of the big cats, the best climbers are the jaguar, which lives in Central and South America, and the leopard, which lives in Africa and Asia. The jaguar is the bigger of the two and is the largest cat in the Americas. Like the tiger, it prowls through forests and grasslands, ambushing prey.

NIGHT PROWLER
Jaguars hunt mainly after dark. They sometimes rest on low branches by day, and will occasionally pounce on monkeys and other tree-dwellers.

TUCKED AWAY

Apart from cheetahs, all cats can fold the fingers on their paws to tuck their claws inside their fur.

FLICK KNIVES

Covering the claws keeps them sharp. Cats expose their claws only when hunting or climbing trees.

Spot the Leopard

The leopard's spotted coat makes it hard to see when it is creeping through high grass or perched in the branches of a tree. Leopards spend long periods in trees, where it is often cooler and they are safe from predators. They hunt alone, often at night, and will eat all kinds of meat. Favorite titbits include gazelles, jackals, baboons, storks, rodents, reptiles, and even fish.

A ROARING SUCCESS
The leopard's ability to eat a wide range of food has helped it thrive. It is common in Africa and southern Asia.

HIGH AND DRY
Leopards have strong neck and back muscles that help them drag prey up into trees, away from scavengers.

The Fastest Thing on Four Legs

Two things help the cheetah stand out from the crowd of other cats. First, it does not have retractable claws. Second, it can outrun not only all other cats, but every other creature on Earth. Over short distances, it hits speeds of up to 70 miles per hour (110 km/h)—as fast as a car on a freeway. This helps it catch fleet-footed animals such as gazelles and wildebeest, and avoid its main predator, the lion.

Where the cheetah lives in Africa and the Middle East

A SPRING IN ITS STEP
The cheetah has a springlike spine that coils and uncoils as it runs, helping to propel it forward. Its long, streaming tail acts like a rudder on a boat, keeping it going in the right direction.

RUNNING OUT OF STEAM
If a cheetah fails to catch its prey within a distance of about 1,500 feet (450 m), it usually runs short of breath and has to abandon the chase.

Ocelot approaches prey slowly and unseen.

Moves within striking distance.

Suddenly leaps into the air.

Small but Deadly

Small wild cats can be found on all of the continents except for Australia and Antarctica. Some, like the mountain lion and the bobcat of North America, are actually quite large. Others, such as the South American oncilla, are smaller than pet cats. Cats first became pets in Egypt, about 7,000 years ago, when people realized they helped control pests such as mice and rats.

JACK IN THE BOX
When hunting, small cats usually creep along, low to the ground. Then they spring up, falling on their prey and killing it with a bite to the neck.

Kills with a single bite.

Lands on its prey.

The Nine Lives of a Cat

Cats seem to have an amazing ability to escape tricky situations—so much so that people say they have nine lives! In fact, it has more to do with their strength, quick reflexes, and sharp senses. Cats are muscular but agile. Both eyes face forward, which helps them judge distances, and they see well in the dark—six times better than humans. They can also hear faint and high-pitched sounds from far away.

SMALL AND SWIFT
The caracal, which lives in Africa and southwestern Asia, is the fastest small cat. It can jump as high as 10 feet (3 m) to snatch birds from the air.

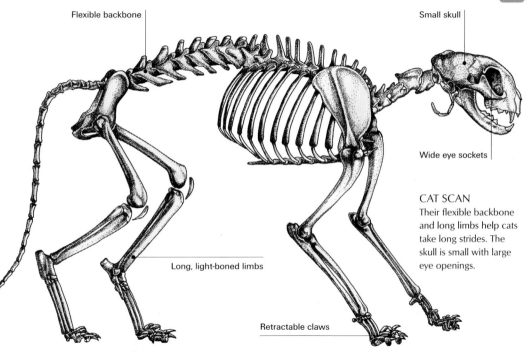

Flexible backbone

Small skull

Wide eye sockets

Long, light-boned limbs

Retractable claws

CAT SCAN
Their flexible backbone
and long limbs help cats
take long strides. The
skull is small with large
eye openings.

Doglike Cats

Hyenas look like dogs, but are more closely related to cats. There are four species: the aardwolf and the brown, spotted, and striped hyenas. All four live in Africa, though the striped hyena is also found in Asia. Hyenas have massive jaws and sharp teeth that can crunch through bones. Unlike most mammals, they can swallow and digest skin and bone.

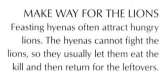

MAKE WAY FOR THE LIONS
Feasting hyenas often attract hungry lions. The hyenas cannot fight the lions, so they usually let them eat the kill and then return for the leftovers.

TEAM WORK
Hyenas often eat meat left behind by other predators, but they also hunt. Spotted hyenas work together to bring down large animals such as gazelles.

Dogs of the Wild

Wolves and wild dogs are meat-eaters and very efficient hunters. They are fast runners and have excellent hearing and sight, as well as a keen sense of smell that helps them sniff out prey. Their jaws are equipped with sharp, pointed canine teeth and scissor-like molar teeth that are ideal for tearing flesh.

AN EERIE CHORUS
Wolves live in groups called packs. They communicate using facial expressions and sounds, including howling. Pack members howl together to warn other packs to keep away.

Clever Canines

There are 34 species of wild dogs, including wolves, foxes, jackals, and coyotes. Dogs have adapted to all kinds of environments and can be found in hot deserts, grasslands, forests, mountains, and the snowy wastes of the Arctic. Some have even adapted to living close to humans.

WILY COYOTES
Coyotes live all over North America, even in large cities like Los Angeles.

Where wolves and wild dogs live

DID YOU KNOW?

Today's domestic dogs, or pet dogs, are descended from wolves.

PLIGHT OF THE WOLF

Because they kill sheep and cattle, gray wolves have been widely hunted. They now live only in remote areas of the Northern Hemisphere.

On the Prowl

Wild dogs have learned many ways to find food. Large wild dogs and wolves usually hunt in packs. They select a victim then chase and surround it. This way they can hunt animals much larger than themselves. Smaller species, such as foxes and jackals, are more likely to live and hunt in small groups or pairs. They feed on small creatures, fruits, and even human garbage.

MANED WOLF

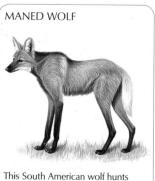

This South American wolf hunts small animals at night and eats fruits.

RED WOLF

The rare North American red wolf eats deer, raccoons, and rabbits.

DINGO

Dingoes live in Australia, where they hunt kangaroos and wallabies.

Communication

Wolves and other wild dogs communicate with each other, and with other animals, in a range of ways. They recognize each other by their smells, and they mark their territories with their urine and dung. They bark, howl, squeal, whimper, and growl to express feelings, warnings, and directions. And they also use facial expressions and tail and body postures to send clear messages.

COYOTE FACE: ATTACKING

Ears up, teeth bared

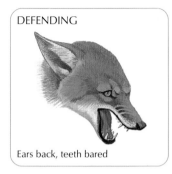

DEFENDING

Ears back, teeth bared

WOLF TAIL: THREATENING

Tail high, fur fluffed out

READY TO ATTACK

Tail straight out

FRIENDLY

Ears relaxed, mouth closed

PLAYFUL

Ears alert, mouth relaxed

SUBMISSIVE

Ears down, mouth closed

FEARFUL

Tail touches belly.

RELAXED

Tail held loosely.

SUBMISSIVE

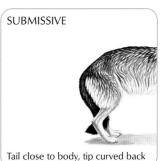

Tail close to body, tip curved back

Coping with Cold

Among the most specialized dog species are those that live in high mountains and the Arctic. They have developed a range of adaptations to cold, snowy climates. Gray wolves grow thick coats for winter and have paws that move easily through snow and grip well on ice. The coat of the arctic fox changes from brown or black to white in winter, to camouflage it in the snow.

Where the arctic fox lives

WINTER COAT
The arctic fox's white coat is thicker than its dark summer coat, and is especially dense around its paws.

LENDING A PAW
Dogs have been trained to do all sorts of tasks. In the Arctic, people use dogs called huskies to pull sleds.

DID YOU KNOW?
Dogs were the first animals to become pets—about 14,000 years ago.

Meat and Only Meat

Most wild dogs will eat a range of foods to survive, but the Cape wild dog, also called the African hunting dog, likes meat and only meat. It lives in the woodlands and grasslands of East Africa, where packs of between 2 and 40 hunting dogs work together to catch prey as large as gazelles and wildebeest.

FIGHT FOR THE RIGHT

Males compete for the right to breed with the dominant female.

CARING AND SHARING

Adult dogs often regurgitate meat for young or sick dogs to eat.

Where the Cape wild dog lives

COAT OF MANY COLORS
Cape wild dogs may appear dark or fairly light in color, depending on the pattern on their coat. Every dog has a different pattern.

Scare Bears

Bears are among the biggest and strongest meat-eaters on land. They have a powerful body, long claws, and sharp teeth. But, with the exception of the polar bear, bears spend more time feeding on plants, berries, insects, and honey than they do hunting animals. Bears usually keep away from humans, but may attack people who get too close, especially when the bears are guarding their cubs.

SNIFF AND SCRATCH
Bears use their keen sense of smell to find food hidden in burrows or nests, and their sharp claws to dig it out.

GIANT ANCESTOR
The giant short-faced bear roamed North America between 2 million and 10,000 years ago. It was the largest meat-eating mammal that ever lived.

93

The Average Bear

Most bears share the same overall shape. They have a large
head, broad shoulders, a stocky body, thick legs and arms, and
a short tail. Normally, they walk on all four feet, but they can
rise up and even walk on their back legs. This makes them look
even bigger and stronger, which helps scare off rivals. It also
helps them reach up high for food and climb trees.

INDIVIDUAL STYLE

Black bears have hooklike claws
(above left) for climbing trees. The
L-shaped pad on a panda's foot
(above right) helps it grip bamboo.

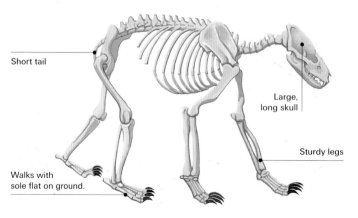

Short tail

Large,
long skull

Sturdy legs

Walks with
sole flat on ground.

FLAT FOOTED
Unlike big cats, which run on their
toes, bears (like humans) walk with
their feet placed flat on the ground.

EASY DOES IT
Because they are so strong, bears have few predators. That means they can amble along at their own slow pace.

Chilling Out

Bears live mainly in the Northern Hemisphere. Those that live in the cold regions of the far north tend to be bigger and more common than the bears that live farther south. When the weather is very cold, bears often retreat to a den and sleep for long periods. During this time, their heart and breathing rates drop to save energy, and they live entirely off their body fat.

DID YOU KNOW?

A panda eats the equivalent of two-fifths of its weight in bamboo every day.

RARE BEARS
There are only about 1,000 pandas left in the wild. They live in the mountains of China, and feed mainly on bamboo.

TOP BUNK

Black bears live in the forests of North America. They often sleep on branches high up in trees, especially when humans are around. All black bears have a brown muzzle, but their coat can vary from light brown to black.

GIANT HELPINGS

The North American form of the brown bear is known as the grizzly bear. It fishes in rivers for salmon and sometimes hunts moose and caribou.

Secretive Southerners

Southern bears are smaller and rarer than their northern relatives. They are shy, but can be aggressive if disturbed. They range in size from the chunky Asiatic black bear, which is as tall as an adult human but twice as heavy, to the little red panda, which is just 19 inches (48 cm) tall.

QUITE A SPECTACLE
The spectacled bear is South America's only bear. It is named for the rings around its eyes.

SWEET TOOTH
The red panda eats meat occasionally, but its favorite foods are bamboo and fruits. It eats mainly at night.

WHITE FRIGHT
The Asiatic black bear feeds mainly at night. To scare off foes, it rears up and displays its bright white chest band.

TICKLISH TREATS
The sloth bear of India and Sri Lanka eats only termites. It sucks up the insects through a wide gap in its front teeth.

A Pole Apart

There is no mistaking a polar bear—its white coat sets it apart from all other members of the bear family. And that's not the only difference between it and its relatives. Most bears live in woodlands, but the polar bear inhabits the frozen shores and seas around the North Pole. And while other bears eat a range of foods, the polar bear feeds almost exclusively on meat.

CONSTANT CARE
Mothers must guard their cubs carefully, for male polar bears often eat them. The cubs stay with their mother for about two years.

KITTED OUT
To keep warm, a polar bear has a thick layer of fat and dense fur that traps heat. Its wide paws grip well on snow and ice and help it swim.

101

A Patient Predator

The polar bear is the largest land-based meat-eater in the world. As well as foraging on land, it hunts efficiently on ice and in water. Its favorite food is seals, mainly ringed or bearded seals. It normally catches them by waiting patiently beside holes in the ice where the seals have to come up every so often to breathe. As soon as the seal pops up, the bear pounces.

GOING UNDER
Polar bears can swim well and will even dive underwater to catch fish and small whales like this beluga.

DID YOU KNOW?

Even an experienced polar bear might catch a seal only once every four or five days.

COMPETING FOR MATES
Fights between males over mating rights can be ferocious. They often result in the death of one bear.

TEETH AND CLAWS: CREATURES OF THE SKY AND SEA

Prehistoric Predators

During the time of the dinosaurs, the skies were ruled by flying, meat-eating lizards, called pterosaurs. Some were as large as a small plane, others as small as today's birds. Sharp-toothed predators also swam in the seas, rivers, and lakes. They included large, long-necked creatures called plesiosaurs, and fierce, wide-jawed killers called pliosaurs.

WHERE THE WATER MEETS THE SKY
In Europe during the Jurassic period, creatures such as *Scaphognathus* would glide over land and water, seeking prey. Here, one is diving toward a school of fish being hunted by *Cryptoclidus*, a plesiosaur.

DID YOU KNOW?

A pterosaur known as Quetzalcoatlus had a wing span of 45 feet (14 m).

The Threat from Above

Birds of prey are birds that hunt other animals. There are more than 300 kinds of birds of prey, but they all have at least three things in common: a hooked beak, curved, sharp claws, and keen eyesight. Some swoop down from high in the sky to seize small animals—including other birds—in their sharp claws. Others soar over vast distances searching for animals that have already died, then descend to feast on the carcasses.

DID YOU KNOW?

Birds of prey have eyesight that is up to three times better than ours.

TERROR IN THE TREETOPS

The harpy eagle of South America is so large and powerful that it can swoop through the trees and snatch a howler monkey off a high branch.

Head to Toe

The hooked beak of a bird of prey helps it cut into flesh, while its strong lower jaw supplies extra pulling power. Its large feet and pointed claws (also called talons) provide a very firm grip. They can also deliver a strong, even fatal, blow as a bird lands on its prey. The exact shapes of the beak and feet depend, however, on the way the bird hunts and the kind of prey it catches. Because of this, a huge range of shapes has evolved.

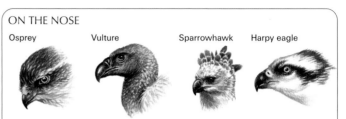

ON THE NOSE

Osprey   Vulture   Sparrowhawk   Harpy eagle

The compact beaks of the osprey, sparrowhawk, and harpy eagle help them handle live prey. The vulture needs a longer beak for probing large carcasses.

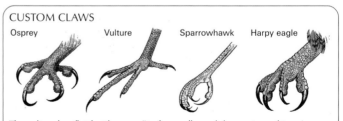

CUSTOM CLAWS

Osprey   Vulture   Sparrowhawk   Harpy eagle

The vulture has flat feet because it often walks and does not need to grip prey. The other birds have hooked claws for catching prey on the move.

Flight feathers:
10 primary feathers

Alula: wing edge that
helps control speed.

Flight feathers:
secondary feathers

Large, forward-facing eyes

Cere: fleshy band
around beak

Hooked beak

COMMON TRAITS
It is not only the shape of beak
and claws that birds of prey
share. Some of the other
features they have in common
are shown here.

Small feathers called
coverts protect base
of flight feathers.

12–14 tail
feathers

Talons

Powerful legs and feet

High Fliers

Condors and vultures from
the New World (North and
South America) make up
one group of birds of prey.
All are scavengers and feed
on dead animals. The New
World vultures look very like
vultures from the Old World
(Europe, Asia, and Africa) but,
surprisingly, are not related.
Instead, they are descended
from storks. The two kinds of
vultures developed similar
features because they hunt
and feed in the same way.

MOUNTAIN DWELLER
The Andean condor is the world's
largest bird of prey. It lives in the
Andes Mountains of South America,
where it nests on ledges and in caves.

Andean condor

Bearded vulture

Secretary bird

White-bellied sea eagle

Rough-legged buzzard

Peregrine falcon

Lesser kestrel

Little sparrowhawk

A BROAD SPAN

The wingspans of birds of prey vary widely. The Andean condor's wingspan is 9½ feet (2.9 m).

SHARING THE SPOILS

Like most vultures, Andean condors spend long periods soaring high in the sky, scanning the ground for food. Condors feed mainly on dead llamas, sheep, and cattle. Vultures often fight over food, but condors are happy to share.

Something for Everyone

The vultures of the Old World (Europe, Asia, and Africa) are part of the largest group of birds of prey, which also includes eagles, hawks, and kites. Vultures come in all sizes, and often the different-sized birds feed on different parts of the same dead animals. The largest vultures usually eat the muscles and intestines, the medium-sized birds eat the skin and tendons, and the smallest vultures clean up the leftovers.

DID YOU KNOW?
Egyptian vultures use large stones to crack open ostrich eggs, then eat the contents.

PARTY ANIMALS

Hundreds of vultures, such as these Rüppell's griffon vultures, may gather around a single dead animal. Some simply gather to meet other vultures.

SPACIOUS ACCOMMODATION

The lappet-faced vulture lives in dry areas of Africa. Its nest measures up to 6½ feet (2 m) across—wide enough for an adult human to lie down in it!

Symbols of Power

Eagles live on all the continents except Antarctica. Of all the birds of prey, they are perhaps the most admired by humans. Their great size, strong but elegant bodies, fierce facial expressions, and impressive hunting skills have led to their images being used on symbols of power such as flags, crests, military badges and medals, and business logos.

AMERICAN ICON
The majestic bald eagle was chosen as the national bird of the United States of America in 1782. The second choice was the wild turkey!

WHERE DID IT GO?
Bald eagles hunt mainly by swooping on fish. Not every dive is successful. They also feed on ducks and carrion, and may steal food from other birds.

Expert Anglers

Sea eagles and ospreys are found in many parts of the world. They specialize in catching fish. Normally they do this by diving suddenly to snatch fish from near the surface of the water. Most have strong toes and tightly curved talons to help them grasp their prey. The most successful fisher, and one of the most efficient birds of prey, is the osprey. It has a strike rate of nine catches for every ten dives.

IN FREE FALL

A hunting osprey flies in a figure eight over water. When it spies a fish, it drops rapidly, feet first.

UP, UP, AND AWAY

Skimming the water, the osprey hooks the fish with its talons, then pulls up, carrying off its prize.

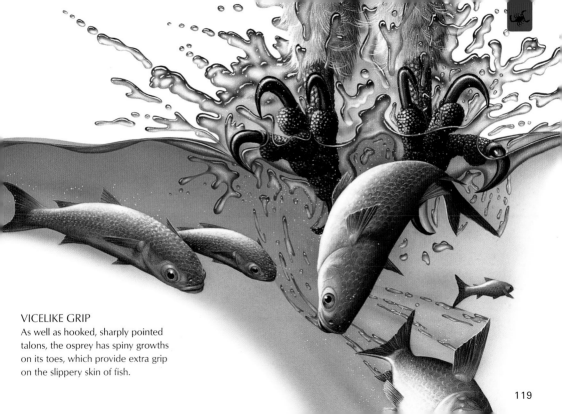

VICELIKE GRIP
As well as hooked, sharply pointed
talons, the osprey has spiny growths
on its toes, which provide extra grip
on the slippery skin of fish.

Surprise Attacks

Falcons are not the biggest birds of prey, but what they lack in size they more than make up for in speed. Most falcons catch other birds by dropping on them from above, often in midair. They fall so fast and from such a great height that the prey does not even have time to react. The fastest falcon, the peregrine falcon, can dive at speeds of up to 200 miles per hour (320 km/h).

EYE IN THE SKY
Kestrels, like this white-eyed kestrel, spend long periods hovering in the sky, looking for prey on the ground.

FROM OUT OF NOWHERE

Plummeting from above like a stone, a peregrine falcon stuns a Eurasian oystercatcher with a blow from its feet, then catches it as it falls.

Night Raiders

It can get a little crowded in the daytime skies, and there is not always enough prey to go round. So some meat-eating birds sleep by day and hunt by night. Owls find mice and other small animals using their sharp hearing and powerful night vision that allows them to see well in the dark. Then they swoop in silence so that the prey does not hear them until it is too late.

MIDNIGHT OWL
The barn owl is common in many parts of the world. Its hearing is so good that it can find prey in total darkness, guided only by sounds.

IN FOR THE KILL

An owl pins its prey with its claws, then kills it with a bite to the neck.

GOOD LOOKING

binocular vision

full range of vision

Binocular vision—seeing with both eyes—helps an owl judge distance.

Mammals on the Wing

Bats first took to the air 50 million years ago, and are still the only mammals capable of powered flight. Their wings have helped them spread to most parts of the world, and there are now almost 1,000 species of all shapes and sizes. Bats are active mainly at night. Some eat only fruits, but most catch insects. A few prey on larger animals—and even drink their blood!

SAFETY IN NUMBERS
Bats usually live in dark spaces such as hollow trees, caves, and tunnels. Free-tailed bats like these can form giant colonies of up to 100 million bats.

Seeing with Sound

Most insect-eating bats use a skill called echolocation to find their way about in the dark and catch fast-moving prey. It is a bit like radar. The bat sends out a series of high-pitched calls or clicks and listens to their echoes. The strength of the echoes tells the bat how far away an object is. Changes in the echoes indicate the object's size and even which way it is moving.

SEEK AND DESTROY
These pictures show how a bat uses echolocation to catch its prey.

CONVENTIONAL CALLS

Many bats, such as the whiskered bat, emit calls through their mouth.

A NOSE FOR PREY

Some bats, such as the trident bat, send out sounds via their nose.

Bat makes a series of rapid clicks or calls.

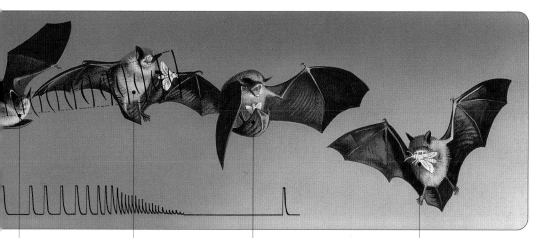

Clicks bounce off insect and back to bat, telling it where prey is.

As the bat gets nearer prey, rate of echoes increases.

Bat zeroes in on prey and seizes it in its claws.

The bat transfers the prey to its mouth.

Fine Tuning

Like all hunters, insect- and meat-eating bats have developed body parts and techniques that help them track down and catch prey. Their strong, flexible wings allow them to move quickly, even in narrow spaces. As well as echolocation, most bats have large ears to help them locate prey. Many have small but sharp teeth, and some have long claws for gripping food.

The large ears of the long-eared bat probably improve its echolocation.

FISH SNATCHER
The South American greater bulldog bat uses its sharp claws to snatch up fish. It can store food in its large cheek pouches.

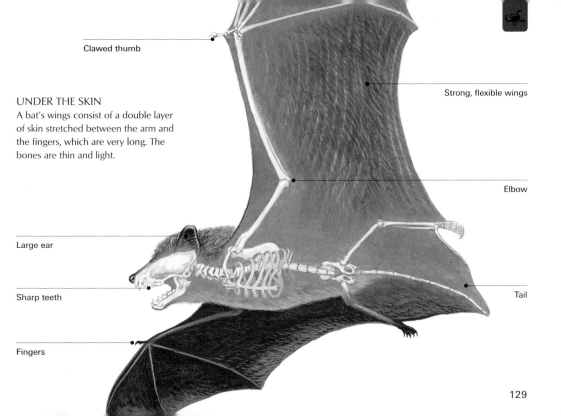

Clawed thumb

Strong, flexible wings

UNDER THE SKIN

A bat's wings consist of a double layer of skin stretched between the arm and the fingers, which are very long. The bones are thin and light.

Elbow

Large ear

Sharp teeth

Tail

Fingers

Thirst for Blood

Some of the large insect-eating bats also catch fish, frogs, birds, and other small animals. But the most notorious hunters among bats are the vampire bats, which drink blood from live, often large animals. A vampire bat does this by sneaking up to an animal and nipping it with its sharp teeth. It then laps up the flow of blood, often without the animal noticing.

LET IT FLOW

The common vampire bat's long, pointed teeth are razor sharp. Its saliva contains substances that stop blood clotting, causing cuts to bleed more and for longer.

DID YOU KNOW?

Vampire bats often regurgitate blood to feed hungry companions.

Where the vampire bat lives

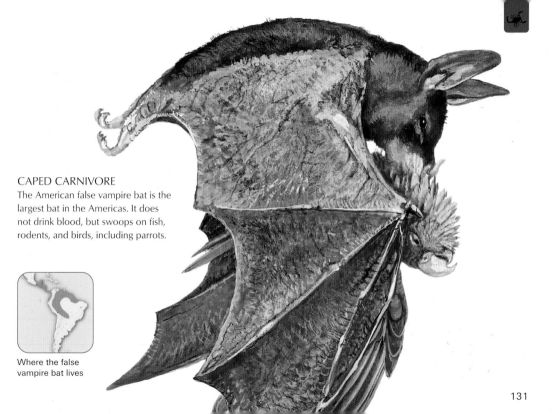

CAPED CARNIVORE
The American false vampire bat is the largest bat in the Americas. It does not drink blood, but swoops on fish, rodents, and birds, including parrots.

Where the false vampire bat lives

131

Never Smile at a Crocodile

The biggest, fiercest reptiles on the planet are crocodiles and alligators—or crocodilians, as they are also known. King of the crocs is the saltwater crocodile, which can measure 23 feet (7 m) in length—about the length of four adult humans lying head to toe. Small crocodilians eat fish, insects, and small mammals. The largest species kill and eat animals as big as horses, cattle—and people!

HEAVYWEIGHT CHALLENGER
Found in central and southern Africa, the Nile crocodile can weigh as much as 14 adult humans. It is aggressive and often attacks people and boats.

Lying in Wait

Crocodilians are lazy hunters. They spend long periods floating in water, not moving but just waiting for food to come to them. They lie just below the surface, so that little of their body is visible. When prey passes close enough, the crocodilian attacks suddenly and ferociously. It grabs the animal in its massive jaws, and pulls it under the water to drown it before eating it.

CROC FLAP
A flap of skin at the back of its mouth stops water going down a crocodile's throat. This allows it to hold prey under water but still breathe.

UNDER THE SURFACE
A crocodile's eyes, ears, and nose are positioned so that they remain above the surface while the rest of its body is under water.

Energy Savers

Crocodilians are cold blooded. That means they control the temperature of their body by moving in and out of warm and cold places. For most crocodiles and alligators, that involves moving in and out of water. To warm up, they move onto land to bask in the sun. To cool down, they return to the water. Their exact routine depends on the climate where they live.

STAYING WARM IN THE COLD
In cold areas, alligators may stay under water to avoid freezing weather. They breathe through a hole in the ice.

RESTING UP
The bodies of crocodilians are large, but float easily. That allows them to save their energy for launching sudden attacks on prey.

DID YOU KNOW?
A crocodilian can survive for months without a meal, due to its efficient use of energy.

Walk Like a Croc

Crocodilians move more easily in water, but can also get around on land. On slippery surfaces, they often slide on their belly. To cover longer distances on dry land, they lift themselves up on their short, straight legs and walk—awkwardly but steadily. Crocodilians cannot, however, climb trees, which is worth remembering if you are ever chased by one!

GOING THE DISTANCE
Some crocodilians, such as the common caiman, will walk for many miles to find new hunting territories.

COMMANDO CRAWL

To hide themselves from prey or predators, crocodilians crawl low to the ground, with their feet spread wide.

STRAIGHT IS THE GAIT

When they walk high, crocodilians hold their legs in an almost vertical position, directly under their body.

HIGH JUMP
Using its tail to push itself upward, an alligator can launch itself far out of the water to snatch small animals and birds from riverbanks and trees.

BURSTS OF SPEED

Some crocodilians, such as the Australian freshwater crocodile, can break into a gallop.

Messy Eaters

A crocodilian's teeth are designed for grabbing and holding prey rather than cutting and chewing. So crocodilians have to swallow prey whole, or at best break it into large chunks by shaking it violently. To help them digest their food, crocodilians' stomachs have two sections. The first section contains stones that help break down the food. The second is a normal stomach.

ARMOR PLATED
Crocodilians have small bones called osteoderms under the thick scales on their back. They protect them from bites from predators or rival crocs.

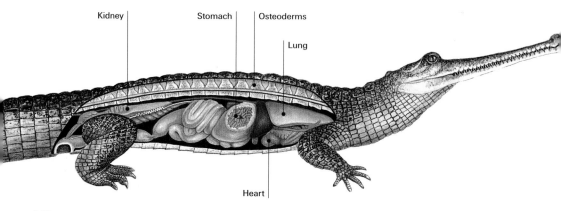

Kidney

Stomach

Osteoderms

Lung

Heart

CONSTANT RENEWAL
Crocodilian teeth are replaced regularly. New teeth come through in waves. Each wave replaces every second tooth. The others are replaced by the next wave.

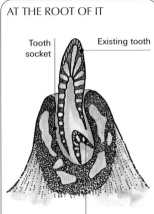

AT THE ROOT OF IT

Tooth socket

Existing tooth

Replacement tooth

New teeth grow inside the tooth sockets of existing teeth. They get steadily larger until they force the old tooth out of the way, then fill the socket.

Guard Duty

Female crocodilians lay eggs, which they normally bury in sand. Often they cover the sand with rotting plant matter, which provides extra warmth. The mother does not leave the nest until the young hatch, between 60 and 100 days later. During this time, she protects the nest fiercely. When she hears the first hatchling emerging, she uncovers the eggs and cracks the shells gently to free the rest.

BABY CARRIER
A mother stays with her hatchlings for several weeks. When they are ready to swim, she carries them carefully in her mouth to water.

Family Snaps

The crocodilians include three main groups or subfamilies: alligators and caimans, crocodiles, and the gharial. There are just two alligator species, the American alligator and the Chinese alligator, and five caimans. Most feed on small animals, but American alligators will occasionally snap up humans, too.

SMALLER PORTIONS

The Cuvier's dwarf caiman of South America snacks on fish and frogs. It has a high skull, like a dog's.

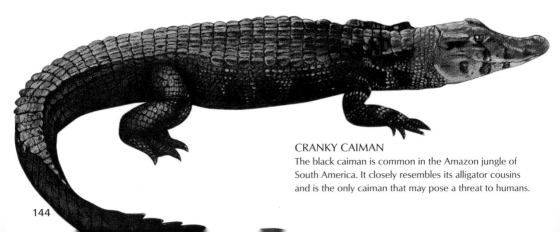

CRANKY CAIMAN
The black caiman is common in the Amazon jungle of South America. It closely resembles its alligator cousins and is the only caiman that may pose a threat to humans.

WINTER HIDEOUT

Chinese alligators dig complex networks of burrows, where they spend much of their time. Like other alligators, they retreat to their dens in winter to hibernate.

Killer Crocs

The largest of the crocodilians are the crocodiles. The 13 species are spread over Central and South America, Africa, Southern Asia, and Australia, where they have a fearsome reputation as predators of humans. By far the most dangerous are the Nile crocodile and the saltwater crocodile. Both are highly aggressive and have taken many human lives. They may prey on people for food, or attack to defend their territory.

DID YOU KNOW?
Saltwater crocodiles have been seen swimming hundreds of miles from land.

ORINOCO
The Orinoco crocodile lives along the Orinoco River in northern South America. Its narrow snout is suited to snapping up fish, but it also eats small mammals.

BLINK AND YOU'LL MISS IT
A saltwater or Indopacific crocodile
may weigh up to 3 tons (2.7 tonnes).
But it can still leap out of water and
gobble up prey in the blink of an eye.

In a Class of Its Own

The gharial subfamily has just one member: the gharial or Indian gharial of Southern Asia. The gharial is easily identified by its long, narrow snout, which is lined with small, sharp teeth. The upper and lower teeth interlock neatly when the jaw is closed. The gharial eats small animals and occasionally large ones, but no attacks on humans have been recorded.

WEAK WALKER
The gharial can grow to a length of 21 feet (6.5 m). It has weak legs and seldom travels far on land.

TRUE OR FALSE?
Scientists do not know how closely related the false gharial is to the gharial. Like gharials, false gharials have long, thin snouts. They live in tropical swamps, lakes, and rivers in Asia.

Head to Head

AMERICAN CROCODILE

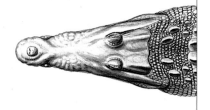

To work out which crocodilian is which, take a look at their heads. You know it is a crocodile if a large tooth on the lower jaw remains visible when its mouth is closed.

AMERICAN ALLIGATOR

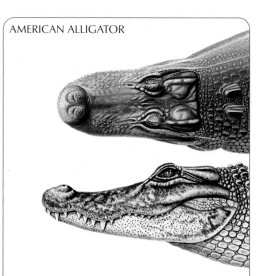

Alligators have a broad snout, which is ideal for catching fish and larger animals. Unlike the crocodiles, their lower teeth all fit neatly inside their mouth when it is closed.

BLACK CAIMAN

Like their close relatives the alligators, caimans also have a broad snout. The skin on the black caiman's head is much more colorful than that of most other crocodilians.

GHARIAL

Especially when viewed from above, the gharial's narrow snout sets it apart from other crocodilians. Snouts like this are useful for poking into burrows to find crabs.

Shark Attack!

The sight of a shark fin slicing through the sea strikes terror into the hearts of swimmers and surfers. Sharks are among the world's most dangerous predators. Attacks on humans do occur and about six people are killed each year. But these attacks are rare, if you consider that millions of people use the sea safely every day. In fact, you are more likely to be struck by lightning than attacked by a shark.

GREAT WHITE KILLER

The great white shark can grow to
a mighty 24 feet (7.3 m) in length.
It is the shark humans fear the most,
though it only rarely preys on people.

A Close Watch

Until recently, people were so afraid of sharks that they would always keep away from them or try to kill them. Today scientists regularly study sharks, partly to learn how to avoid being attacked by them. People can swim safely alongside smaller sharks and watch their behavior, but special equipment is needed for observing large and deadly species.

UNDER OBSERVATION
To get close to large sharks such as great white sharks, scientists dive into their territory in strong steel cages. Often the sharks bite the cage!

WE COME IN PEACE
If a shark feels threatened by a diver, it may attack. So divers have learned to fold their arms to make themselves appear less threatening.

Family Portrait

Although some sharks are as big as a bus, others could fit in your hand. While some have huge, gaping mouths, others have snouts like hammers or saws. Some are a single color; others wear spots and stripes. All sharks have strong tails, at least five pairs of gills, and two sets of side fins. Most also have two fins on their back and one on the belly. Of the 400 or so kinds of sharks, just 27 have attacked people. But all are meat-eating predators.

SHARK SCALES
Sharks come in all sizes. The whale shark can grow to 40 feet (12 m). In contrast, the spined pygmy shark measures just 6 inches (15 cm).

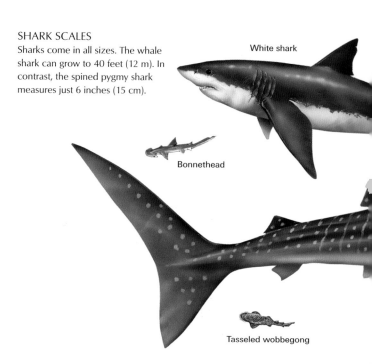

White shark

Bonnethead

Tasseled wobbegong

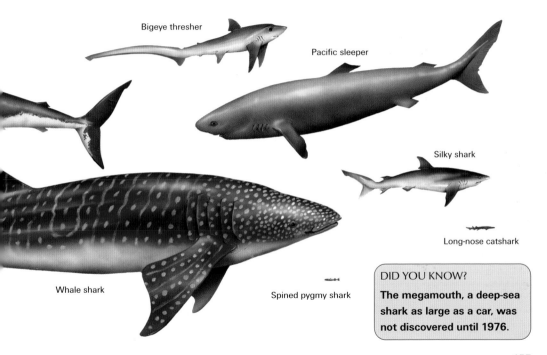

Bigeye thresher

Pacific sleeper

Silky shark

Long-nose catshark

Whale shark

Spined pygmy shark

DID YOU KNOW?

The megamouth, a deep-sea shark as large as a car, was not discovered until 1976.

Open Wide

With no arms or claws to grab their prey, most sharks rely on their massive jaws and sharp teeth to do most of the work when attacking. Normally, a shark's teeth are well hidden inside its mouth. But as it launches itself on its prey, muscles in its face pull its snout back, push its teeth forward, and open its jaws wide. The shark then bites down, shearing off a huge bite, which it swallows whole.

DID YOU KNOW?

The bite of a shark is more than 30 times as powerful than the bite of a human.

WHAT'S ON THE MENU?
This baby albatross has just managed to escape an attacking tiger shark. Seabirds, seals, shellfish, and fish are staple shark foods.

The Cutting Edge

Special adaptations help sharks dominate their watery world. Like other fish, sharks have gills that allow them to absorb oxygen from water. Their skeleton is made of cartilage, which is lighter than bone, and their liver is full of a fatty oil that is lighter than water. Their streamlined, muscular body helps them move at high speed. Shark teeth are regularly replaced and vary in shape according to the food the shark eats.

INSIDE INFORMATION
In many ways a shark's insides are much like ours. They have many of the same organs. Most of the differences are adaptations to underwater life.

A FIRM HOLD

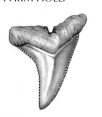

The long, serrated teeth of the blue shark help it catch slippery squid.

GREAT BITES

Great white shark teeth are made for cutting big prey into small bites.

HOOKED FAST

Mako sharks have long, pointed teeth for grabbing hold of prey.

SHELL OPENERS

A tiger shark's sharp, serrated teeth help it cut through turtle shells.

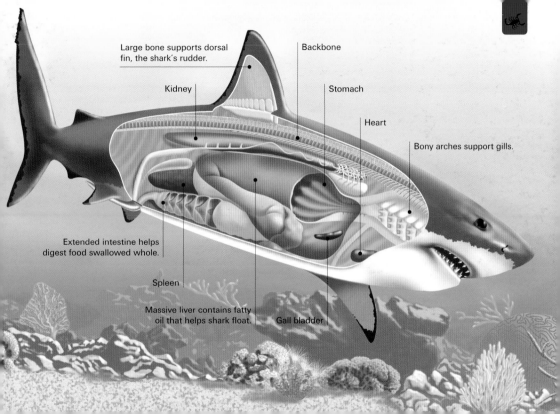

Large bone supports dorsal
fin, the shark's rudder.

Kidney

Backbone

Stomach

Heart

Bony arches support gills.

Extended intestine helps
digest food swallowed whole.

Spleen

Massive liver contains fatty
oil that helps shark float.

Gall bladder

Talking Senses

To help them find prey underwater, where visibility is often poor, sharks have developed keen senses. They can hear low sounds, such as an anchor striking the seabed, from more than 1 mile (1.6 km) away, and they can sniff out the tiniest drops of blood. Their eyes are too far apart to see what is immediately in front of them, but they can still locate prey at close quarters by sensing the electrical charges given off by the creatures.

GOOD VIBRATIONS

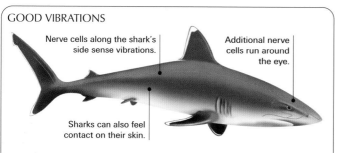

Nerve cells along the shark's side sense vibrations.

Additional nerve cells run around the eye.

Sharks can also feel contact on their skin.

A swimming shark sends out vibrations, which bounce off other objects. It senses the vibrations that bounce back. This tells it where things are.

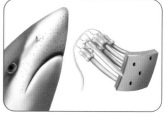

JELLO-VISION
The pores on a shark's snout are connected to the shark's nervous system by a series of jelly-filled tubes.

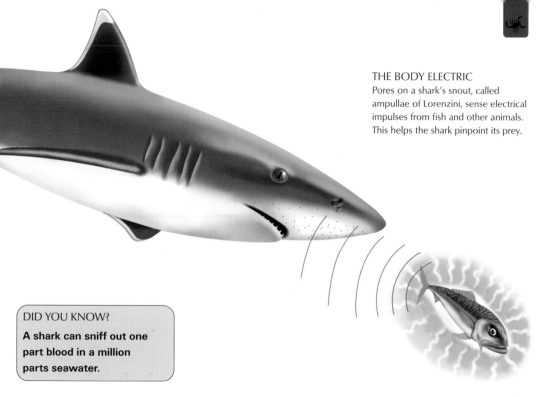

THE BODY ELECTRIC

Pores on a shark's snout, called ampullae of Lorenzini, sense electrical impulses from fish and other animals. This helps the shark pinpoint its prey.

DID YOU KNOW?

A shark can sniff out one part blood in a million parts seawater.

Tail of Destruction

All sharks use their tail to swim and steer, and the exact shape of a shark's tail can tell you something about how it moves and hunts. Symmetrical, crescent-shaped tails usually belong to fast swimmers, while tails with long, thin sections belong to sharks that move more slowly. In the case of the thresher shark, the tail is also a deadly weapon. The thresher uses its extremely long tail to round up and stun or kill fish before eating them.

SLOW AND STEADY

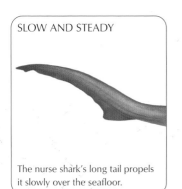

The nurse shark's long tail propels it slowly over the seafloor.

TWIST AND TURN

The long upper section of the tiger shark's tail helps it turn quickly.

FULL STEAM AHEAD

The mako shark's broad, strong tail powers it along at high speed.

THRASHED BY A THRESHER
The thresher has by far the longest tail of any shark. It uses it not only to gather and strike fish but also to scoop them into its mouth.

Eating Methods

To survive, sharks must eat large amounts of food every day—proportionately far more than humans. And they have to do this while avoiding other predators. Almost all sharks use their teeth to eat. But some—the largest sharks—have developed a different way of eating huge quantities of food. They suck in gallons of seawater and strain it through their gills. The gills trap plankton, shrimps, and small fish, which the shark then eats.

DRIFT NET

The basking shark opens its mouth wide to form a huge net for food.

SUPER SCOOPER

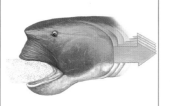

The megamouth drops its lower jaw to scoop up food-filled water.

TAKING THE STRAIN

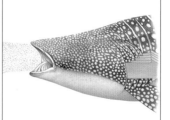

Whale sharks often suck up enormous amounts of plankton.

Head Hunters

Some sharks have what look like two wings on either side of their head. This makes them look like a hammer, so these sharks are called hammerheads. Having a hammer-shaped head makes it easier to swim because water flowing under the wings lifts the shark's head. It makes it easier to hunt, too, because the pores on the shark's head that sense electricity are spread over a larger area. And the hammer comes in very handy for digging up and holding prey!

SCANNING THE SAND

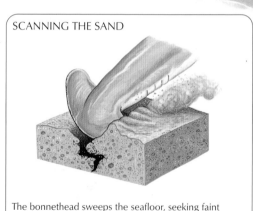

The bonnethead sweeps the seafloor, seeking faint electrical charges emitted by concealed animals. When it senses some, it uses its head to dig out the prey.

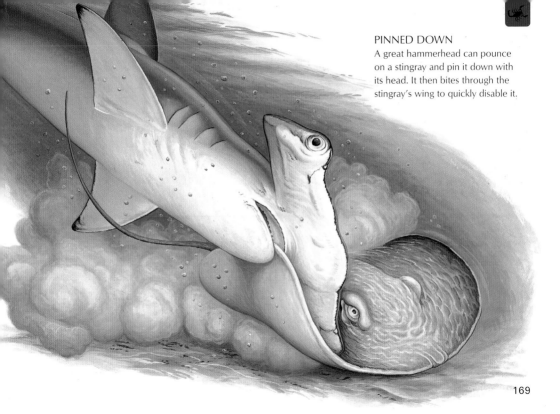

PINNED DOWN
A great hammerhead can pounce on a stingray and pin it down with its head. It then bites through the stingray's wing to quickly disable it.

169

Self Defense

Survival for sharks is not only a matter of eating plenty. It is also about not getting eaten. Young sharks are often gobbled up by larger sharks, dolphins, or whales. Their mothers offer little protection, because they abandon their eggs after laying them. To avoid predators, some baby sharks hide in caves or coral, and a few species have camouflaged skin. Older sharks may seek safety in numbers, or use threatening postures to try to scare off predators.

WARNING SIGNS

To deter attackers or competitors, the gray reef shark adopts an aggressive posture. It points its front fins down, arches its back, and moves its head from side to side.

MERGING WITH THE BACKGROUND

Zebra sharks are born with a stripy skin that helps hide them from predators on the coral reefs where they live.

SAFE HOUSE

When they need to rest, whitetip reef sharks seek out safe havens such as caves. Often they have to crowd together and share the same small space.

Part of the Scenery

Not all sharks can move quickly enough to pounce on prey. But slow-moving sharks can still surprise prey using strategies other than speed. Some sharks have colors and patterns on their skin that help them blend in with their surroundings—so well that they are almost impossible to spot. This is called camouflage. Passing sea creatures may not even realize that a camouflaged shark is there—until they are snapped up and eaten.

DEADLY DISGUISE
With its patterned skin and fleshy lobes and fringes, the tasseled wobbegong looks just like a rock fringed with marine plants.

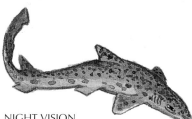

NIGHT VISION
As well as camouflage, catsharks have light-sensitive eyes that let them see in the dark. They pounce on prey with their mouth open and gulp it down.

Clear Danger

One reason why sharks and people meet is that sharks are fond of shallow coastal waters. That is because these waters are rich in food. Marine plants, such as kelp and sea grasses, thrive in the shallows because the sunlight reaches them and plentiful nutrients are washed off the land and onto the seabed by rain and rivers. This attracts hordes of plant-eaters, including fish, turtles, and manatees—all of which offer tasty snacks for sharks!

OUT IN THE OPEN
Shallow waters offer some disadvantages for hungry sharks. The clear water means that prey are more likely to see them coming.

Killer Whales

Whales are the largest creatures on Earth. The biggest, the blue whale, is the size of 26 African elephants, and its heart alone is as big as a car. But although they have been known to ram boats, most large whales are filter feeders and seldom attack large animals or humans. The most ferocious hunters among whales are small species, such as orcas and belugas, which pursue and kill fish, squid, and even large marine mammals.

BREAKING UP THE PARTY

Orcas hunt in packs to catch large fish and squid. They also launch themselves onto beaches to snap up unsuspecting seals and sea lions.

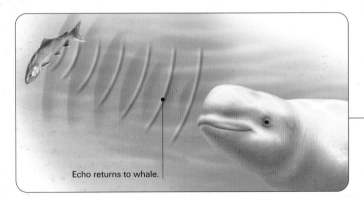

Echo returns to whale.

HEARING A SHAPE

Like bats, small whales use a kind of radar called echolocation to find food. They send out clicks, and listen to the echoes to work out where prey is.

Fish Hooks

Sharks and whales are not the only underwater predators with sharp teeth. Many eels, such as moray eels, have wide jaws filled with long, pointed teeth, and have been known to bite divers. Some deep-sea fish, such as dragonfish, have teeth that are huge compared to their bodies. In fresh water, fish called pikes are among the fiercest hunters. Their needle-like lower teeth slice easily through flesh, while their hooklike upper teeth prevent prey escaping.

HIGH-SPEED CHASE
Barracudas can grow as large as an adult human, and have enormous dagger-like teeth. They often charge in a large group at huge schools of fish.

VENOMOUS CREATURES OF THE LAND

Lethal Liquids

Many creatures use poisons or venoms to kill or subdue their prey. In most cases, the venom is injected through the teeth when the animal bites, but it can also be carried on spines, claws, and even skin. Among the most venomous of creatures on land are spiders. Most spiders use poison that is harmless to humans, but deadly to smaller animals. Others carry venom that is so toxic that they can kill a human with a single bite.

CHOICE OF WEAPONS
The Mexican red-kneed tarantula can usually kill with a bite of its large fangs. If that is not enough, it can also inject a deadly venom into its prey.

SPITTING DISTANCE
The spitting spider shoots streams of sticky, paralyzing venom at its prey from a distance. It then moves in on its disabled victim.

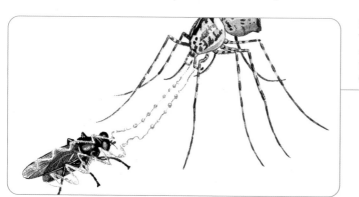

Toxic Terrors

All spiders are meat-eating predators and most produce poison. But of the 35,000 or so kinds of spiders in the world, only about 30 have venom that is really harmful to humans. Most poisonous spider bites can now be treated with medicines called antivenins. So, as long as they can get to hospital in time, most people now survive even the nastiest of spider bites.

DID YOU KNOW?

The venom of a redback spider is 15 times more toxic than that of a rattlesnake.

IN AND OUT

Most spiders bite by moving their fangs inward, toward each other.

DOWN AND UP

Other spiders, especially large, hairy ones, bite downward.

RED SPELLS DANGER
A redback spider uses its sharp fangs to hold its prey while its venom starts to work. The poison paralyzes the victim and eventually causes death.

Storing Venom

Spiders store venom in glands inside their fangs. When a spider bites its prey, muscles in these glands squeeze the poison out through tubes that lead to small holes at the end of the fangs. Spiders cannot eat solid food, so they have to turn their victim into liquid before slurping it up. Some do this by mashing the prey with their strong mouthparts. But most do it by spitting digestive juices onto their victim. These slowly turn the body into a soft mush.

PACKING A POISON

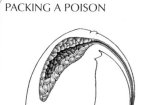

Glands inside a spider's fangs hold venom and digestive juices.

THE INSIDE STORY
Spiders have similar organs to those we have, such as a heart and brain. Features unique to spiders include the spinnerets, which spin spider silk.

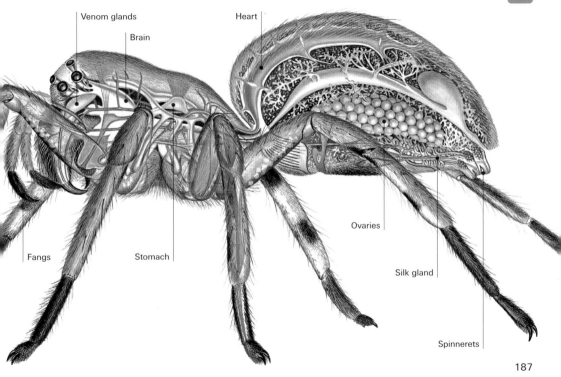

Venom glands

Brain

Heart

Fangs

Stomach

Ovaries

Silk gland

Spinnerets

Closing In

Few spiders rely on eyesight alone to find their prey, particularly as most spiders hunt in the dark. All have two sense organs at the front of their body, called pedipalps, which they use to feel and hold objects. Many also have tiny hairs on their legs, which are attached to sensitive nerves. A movement nearby creates vibrations that make the hairs move. The nerves then pass a message to the brain that danger—or dinner—is on its way.

ON OUR SIDE

Like most spiders, the marbled orb weaver is more of a help than a danger to humans. It eats huge numbers of pests such as flies and cockroaches.

NIGHT VISION

The huge eyes of the ogre-faced spider help it see in the dark.

SHARP EYES

The huntsman spider's spread-out eyes give it good all-round vision.

CLOSE UP

The crab spider usually senses vibrations before it sees its prey.

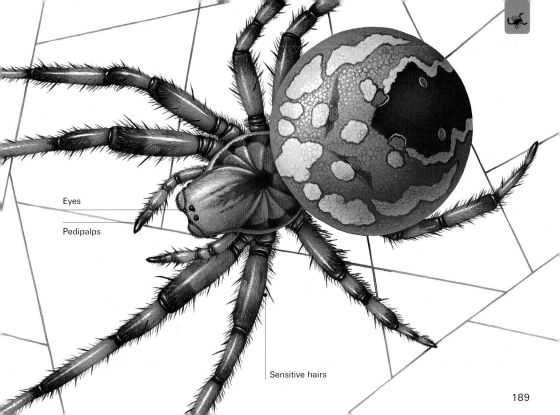

Eyes

Pedipalps

Sensitive hairs

Body Language

Spiders use their senses not only to find food but also to communicate. Some send messages by tapping on the ground, so that nearby spiders pick up the vibrations. Others produce scents to identify themselves.

HEY, I'M OVER HERE!

To attract a mate, some spiders perform courtship displays. The male wolf spider lifts each of his front legs in turn to attract the attention of the female.

SECRET SIGNAL

The male signature spider plucks out a signal on the web of the much larger female. This lets the female know he would like to mate with her.

DAZZLING WITH COLOR

When a male jumping spider meets a female, he waves his front legs in the air to show off his colors and patterns. If the female is impressed, they mate.

Setting a Trap

To capture prey, most spiders make webs. The silk gland in their abdomen forms liquid silk. It is squeezed out of the spider's rear end through spinnerets, which weave the silk into long threads. The spider strings these threads between objects such as plants or rocks. Then it lies in wait. When a creature blunders onto the sticky surface of the web, the spider rushes out and snaps it up.

CASTING AROUND
A net-throwing spider weaves its web between its claws to make a kind of net. It then casts the net over its prey.

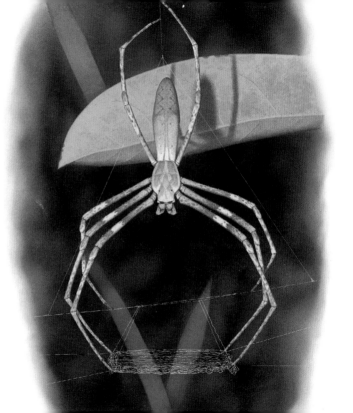

ANCHORING

A spider swings by a thread to connect two objects.

STABILIZING

It strengthens this first thread so that it will support the whole web.

CENTERING

It then joins two dry threads to form the center of the web.

SPOKES OF A WHEEL

Next, the spider runs threads from the center to the edge, like spokes.

TAKING SHAPE

The typical spiral shape of the web is complete. The web is still dry.

A STICKY FINISH

To finish off, the spider adds lines of sticky silk that will trap its prey.

The Webs They Weave

Webs are as varied as the spiders that weave them. Garden spiders make circular, wheel-like webs, whereas house spiders tend to throw together the kind of messy cobwebs you find in the corner of a room or dusty attic. Many ground-dwelling spiders set silk trip wires that alert them to passing prey. Other spiders make complicated webs with two or three layers, so that if the first web fails the second will still trap the victim.

HAMMOCK WEB

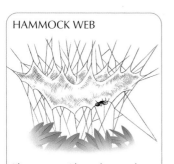

The money spider makes a web with several horizontal layers.

TRIANGULAR WEB

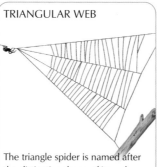

The triangle spider is named after the distinctive shape of its web.

LACY WEB

The lace-web weaver's fine mesh is difficult for insects to escape from.

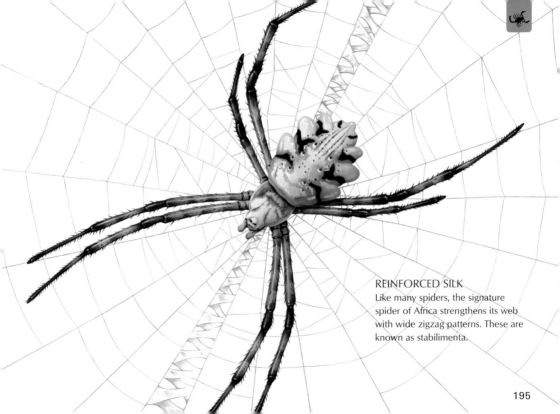

REINFORCED SILK
Like many spiders, the signature spider of Africa strengthens its web with wide zigzag patterns. These are known as stabilimenta.

On the Hunt

Most spiders use their webs to trap food, but some kinds—notably large ground-dwelling spiders—hunt more actively. Many roam alone and often at night. Though some use their speed to run down prey, others rely on surprise as their main weapon. They hide in a corner, then dart out as prey passes. Large fangs and claws and fast-acting venom are especially useful for these spiders because they need to hold and quickly subdue their victim before it wriggles free.

TO HAVE AND TO HOLD

Hunting spiders usually have just two claws at the end of each foot.

WEB GRIPPER

Web-spinners have three claws. The third helps them grip the web.

DID YOU KNOW?

The bolas spider throws a line of sticky silk onto its prey and then reels it in.

READY TO STRIKE

The funnel-web lives in Australia and is one of the world's most venomous spiders. As it closes in on prey, it rears up, ready to strike with its huge fangs.

Look Alikes

If you want to avoid or surprise someone, what better way than to disguise yourself? Or even disappear completely? Some spiders have markings that make them look like something dangerous or unpleasant, so that other creatures will not eat them. Others make themselves almost invisible by using colors and patterns to blend in with their environment. This lets them get close to prey and stay safe from predators.

DROPPING OUT OF SIGHT

The bird-dung spider looks like a bird dropping—not a popular food!

MIMICKING A WASP

This jumping spider from Borneo imitates a wasp with a strong sting.

IMPERSONATING AN ANT

Several spider species look like the types of ants that give a nasty bite.

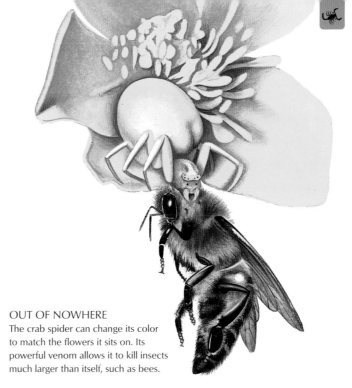

PLAYING DEAD

The scorpion spider hides by pretending to be a dead leaf.

OUT OF NOWHERE

The crab spider can change its color to match the flowers it sits on. Its powerful venom allows it to kill insects much larger than itself, such as bees.

Staying Off the Menu

Spiders are on the menus of many creatures, including birds, lizards, and small mammals. In addition to camouflage, they have developed a range of techniques to avoid being eaten. Ground-dwelling spiders hide in burrows, under rocks, or in holes in buildings. Tarantulas flick spiky hairs at predators. Some spiders will even shed a leg or two to escape capture.

QUICK GETAWAY
The Namibian wheel spider escapes predators such as wasps by curling its legs and rolling away like a wheel. It can move at 3 feet (1 m) per second.

A Sting in the Tail

Scorpions are related to spiders and, like spiders, have eight legs and two feelers at the front of their body, called pedipalps. In scorpions, however, the pedipalps are large claws, similar to those of a crab. Another difference between scorpions and spiders is that scorpions hold venom in their tail rather than in their jaws. A scorpion's tail can deliver a nasty sting, which it uses to disable or kill prey. In some cases, the sting can also kill humans.

DID YOU KNOW?

As many as 5,000 people are thought to die each year from scorpion stings.

DANCE PARTNERS
When preparing to mate, a male and female scorpion hold their stingers up high and grasp claws. They then perform a dance.

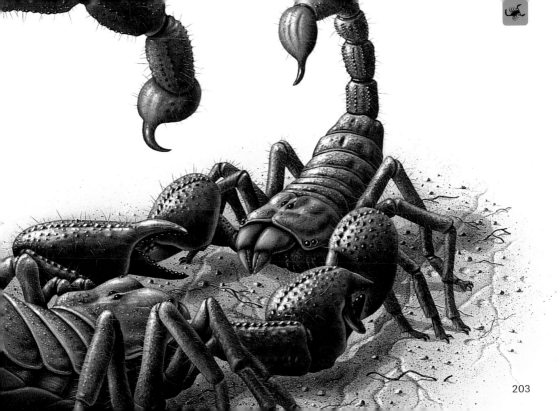

To Sting or Not to Sting?

Scorpions snap up all kinds of small animals, including insects, spiders, snails, lizards, and even rodents. Usually, they lie in wait until they sense vibrations from a passing animal, then rush out to seize it. Larger scorpions grip prey in their claws and sting only if the animal puts up a fight. Smaller scorpions sting almost immediately to make sure the victim does not escape.

DANGER OVERHEAD
To sting, a scorpion arches its tail over its head and quickly brings the pointed stinger down on its prey.

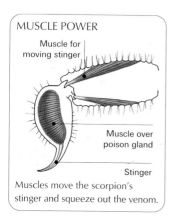

MUSCLE POWER

Muscle for moving stinger

Muscle over poison gland

Stinger

Muscles move the scorpion's stinger and squeeze out the venom.

WHEN THE SUN GOES DOWN
Scorpions hunt alone and mainly between dusk and dawn. By day, they rest under rocks, logs, or bark, or inside their burrows.

Snakes Alive!

Mention the words "poison" and "dangerous" and the first animal most people think of is a snake. There are about 3,000 different kinds of snakes. All feed on other animals, though their choice of food varies widely, from tiny insects to animals as large as goats. Many use venom to paralyze or kill their prey. Some venomous snakes can also kill humans, but almost all will hide from people, and strike only when they feel threatened.

POTENT POISON
Venomous snakes, such as rattlesnakes, usually strike and grab prey with their long fangs, then inject poison to disable or kill the animal.

206

Legless Lizards

Snakes are long, slender reptiles with no legs—rather like legless lizards. Instead of walking, they slide along on their bellies, by pushing against the ground with muscles attached to the underside of their ribs. They can also use these muscles to help them rear up and strike at prey. Although they have teeth, snakes cannot chew, so they must swallow food whole. Digesting large animals can take many days, or even weeks.

STRETCHING TO FIT
Many of a snake's internal organs are long and thin to match its shape. Most snakes have just one lung, whereas other vertebrates have two.

Venom gland

Forked tongue

Fangs

Liver

Ribs   Lung

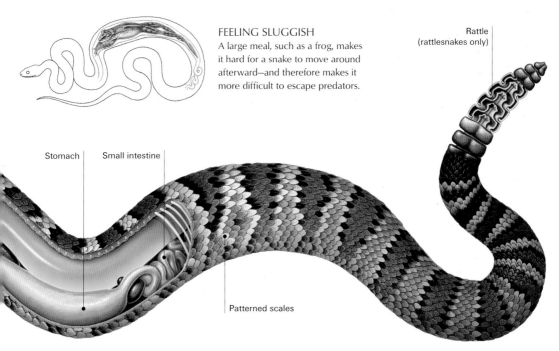

FEELING SLUGGISH

A large meal, such as a frog, makes it hard for a snake to move around afterward—and therefore makes it more difficult to escape predators.

Rattle
(rattlesnakes only)

Stomach

Small intestine

Patterned scales

Sizing Up Snakes

A snake might be only as long as your forearm, or it might be
the length of six men lying end to end—and almost as wide.
But there are three general shapes of snake: small and slender,
short and thick-bodied, and large and shaped like a cylinder.
Small differences in these shapes, and in the shapes of features
such as the head and underside, may tell you something about
how a snake lives and hunts prey.

BIG HEAD	SLIPPING THROUGH	DIGGING DEEP

A python has a big head for holding the teeth it needs to grip prey.	A tree snake has a slender head to allow it to slip between branches.	A blunt, bullet-shaped head helps a burrowing snake push through soil.

Anaconda 33 feet (10 m)

Boa constrictor 14½ feet (4.5 m)

Eastern diamondback rattlesnake
7 feet (2.2 m)

ARROW HEAD

Vipers have wide, triangular heads. The horned viper also has horns.

IT TAKES ALL TYPES
The largest snakes are not necessarily the most dangerous. The yellow-bellied sea snake, for example, is extremely poisonous.

Yellow-bellied sea snake
2½ feet (0.8 m)

DID YOU KNOW?
The country with the highest number of venomous snakes is Australia.

A New Skin

Snake skin is made up of hundreds of scales. These are not separate pieces, but thickened parts of the skin that are connected to other scales by thinner areas of stretchy skin. Some snake skin is smooth, whereas some is rough and scratchy. As snakes grow, their skin becomes too tight, so they regularly shed an old skin to reveal a new one underneath.

TIME FOR A CHANGE
To shed its skin, a snake rubs itself against a rough surface. The old skin then peels off in one long piece.

Keeled scales   Smooth scales   Granular scales

DIFFERENT SCALES
Keeled scales help water snakes steer. Smooth scales allow burrowing snakes to dig. Granular scales help boas grip bark.

A Tight Squeeze

All snakes are meat-eaters but they hunt in different ways. Those that move across the ground feel vibrations that may indicate an animal is nearby. Most see well and use their flickering tongues to "taste" scents in the air— this is especially important for nocturnal snakes, which cannot always see prey. While many snakes use venom to kill prey, others wrap their bodies around animals and squeeze them until they suffocate.

A BIG EATER
A large python can crush and kill large animals, such as a pig. Once the pig is dead, the python stretches its jaws over it until it has swallowed it whole.

Big Mouth Strikes Again

Snakes can swallow animals that are much bigger than they are—indeed, a large python can gulp down a goat or an antelope! How do they do it? The answer is that they have elasticated jaws. Stretchy tendons connect the bones in their jaws, allowing the bones to move far apart when they bite. A snake can also extend its windpipe to the front of its mouth, so that it can keep breathing as it swallows its huge meal.

TIGHT LIPPED

When a snake's mouth is closed, the jaw bones are pulled together.

OPEN WIDE

As a snake opens its mouth, its jaw bones separate.

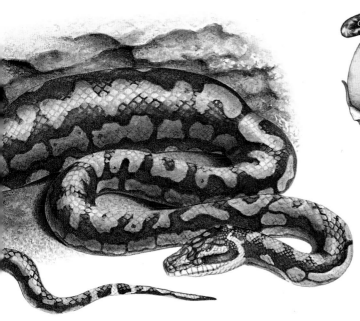

EGG EATERS
African egg-eating snakes use spines inside their bodies to crack eggs open. They then regurgitate the shell.

A PLACE IN THE SUN
After a large meal, a snake often rests in a sunny, sheltered spot. The heat helps it digest its meal more quickly.

What's Your Poison?

Snake venom forms in a gland at the back of the snake's mouth, then passes through tubes called ducts to the teeth. Most snakes have large, hollow fangs at the front of their mouth, which inject the venom into prey. But other snakes have their largest teeth at the back of their mouth. In these snakes, the venom simply runs down grooves in the teeth. When the snake starts to bite, the venom enters the victim.

FIXED FRONT FANGS

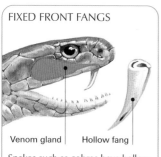

Venom gland | Hollow fang

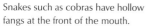

Snakes such as cobras have hollow fangs at the front of the mouth.

SWINGING FRONT FANGS

Venom gland

Hollow fang

The fangs of vipers and rattlesnakes swing forward as the snake strikes.

FIXED REAR FANGS

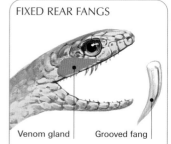

Venom gland | Grooved fang

Fangs at the rear of the mouth are usually fixed and have grooves.

A HOT SHOWER
To defend themselves, spitting cobras spray burning venom into the eyes of predators. When hunting, however, they bite in a normal snake fashion.

Defense Tactics

As they scout around for prey, snakes must also keep an eye out for predators that might eat them. Snakes regularly become snacks for mammals, birds, and reptiles, including other snakes. When it senses danger, a snake might use speed to evade its foe, freeze so that it is hard to spot, or try to make itself look scary by puffing up its body, hissing, and swinging its tail.

THE ART OF DISTRACTION
The rattlesnake uses the rattle on the end of its tail as a decoy. A potential predator or victim will watch the tail rather than the head.

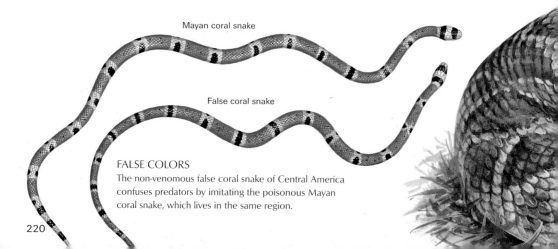

Mayan coral snake

False coral snake

FALSE COLORS
The non-venomous false coral snake of Central America confuses predators by imitating the poisonous Mayan coral snake, which lives in the same region.

Surprise Packages

You might be surprised to learn that some fairly harmless-looking animals are also venomous. For example, a number of shrews—small mouselike mammals—have poisonous saliva. It can kill quite large animals, though it is not harmful to humans. Several tropical frog species carry a deadly venom on their skin to stop predators eating them. And the male platypus has a poisonous spur on each back foot, which it uses to fight off rivals and foes.

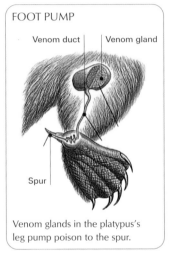

FOOT PUMP

Venom duct | Venom gland

Spur

Venom glands in the platypus's leg pump poison to the spur.

BY A LEG

A platypus can paralyze a person's leg and even kill an animal as large as a dog by wrapping its legs around its attacker and jabbing it with its spurs.

DID YOU KNOW?

The American short-tailed shrew carries enough venom in its saliva to kill 200 mice.

**VENOMOUS
CREATURES
OF THE SKY
AND SEA**

Sting on the Wing

Certain kinds of flying insects use venom. Often it is for defense. Some moths and butterflies, for example, are poisonous to eat. Their bright colors warn predators of this. Bees and wasps sting their attackers, and wasps also sting when hunting. People who are allergic to bee and wasp stings may die if stung. About 100 people a year die this way in the United States alone.

POISON ALERT
The bright coloring of the European wasp warns any would-be attackers that it is dangerous. Wasps are a threat to humans as well as animals.

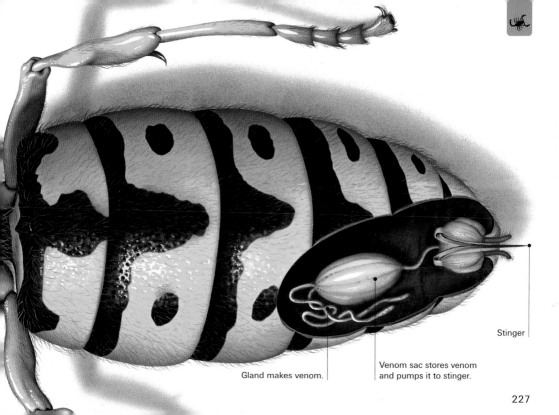

Stinger

Gland makes venom.

Venom sac stores venom and pumps it to stinger.

A Last Resort

Unlike wasps, bees are vegetarians and are not normally aggressive. They sting in self-defense and usually only as a last resort. This is partly because a bee dies soon after it stings. Its stinger has a jagged edge that makes it stay in the victim's skin. When the bee pulls away, the stinger is ripped out, causing an injury that kills it. A few bees have especially dangerous stings: If provoked, a swarm of Southeast Asian honeybees could sting a person to death.

Drone

HIVE OF ACTIVITY
Honeybees live in a hive, often in huge numbers. The hive may contain 80,000 worker bees—females that do not breed—as well as a queen and her drones—the males who mate with her.

Queen bee

Worker bee

Fighting Back

A wasp can inflict a very painful sting—and not just once. Its stinger has smooth sides, allowing it to sting again and again. Some wasps, such as the common wasp, will attack in large swarms when defending their communal nests. The sting of the common wasp is sore, but it is nothing compared to the sting of the North American tarantula hawk wasp, which has been rated the most painful of all.

COMMUNAL LIVING

Social wasps live in large groups. Their nest is started by a queen.

EGG BOXES

The queen lays eggs in cups she makes from chewed wood fibers.

HOME EXTENSIONS

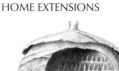

The eggs hatch into worker wasps, who continue to expand the nest.

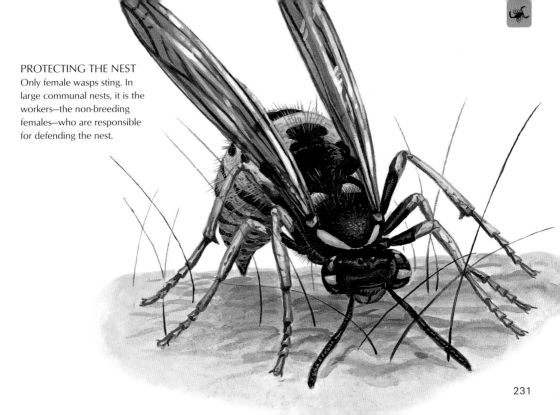

PROTECTING THE NEST
Only female wasps sting. In large communal nests, it is the workers—the non-breeding females—who are responsible for defending the nest.

Making Sense of the World

Like humans, bees and wasps use smell, touch, taste, sight, and hearing to help them move around, find food, and avoid danger. Their eyes consist of thousands of small lenses, each of which records a slightly different view—the brain assembles an overall picture. Hairs on their bodies detect movement and changes in temperature. But most important of all are the antennae, through which bees and wasps hear, feel, and smell.

Tiny hairs detect heat and movement.

The tubelike heart pumps blood around the body.

The last stage of digestion occurs in the stomach.

Insects breathe through air holes called spiracles.

DID YOU KNOW?

The fairyfly wasp is so small that it could fly through the eye of a needle.

INSIDE OUT

This cross-section shows the wasp's internal organs. The breathing system is colored light blue, the digestive system green, the blood circulation red, and the nerves and brain dark blue.

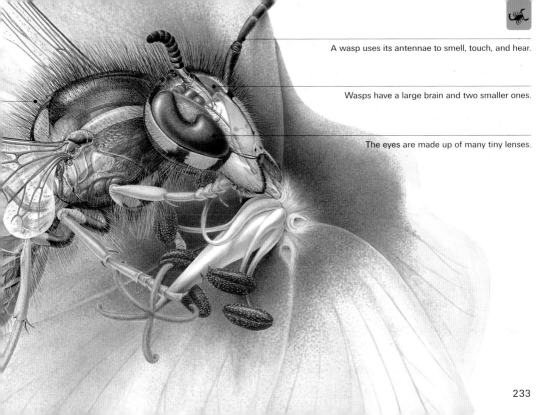

A wasp uses its antennae to smell, touch, and hear.

Wasps have a large brain and two smaller ones.

The eyes are made up of many tiny lenses.

233

Solitary Specialists

The best-known wasps are social wasps, such as common wasps and hornets, which live in nests with large numbers of other wasps. But most wasps are solitary—they live alone in a small nest, usually in the ground. Here the female lays her eggs. She then hunts insects, paralyzes them with her sting, and brings them to the nest for her young to feed on. Many solitary wasps eat just one type of food, such as caterpillars, bees, or spiders.

DRILLER KILLER
The female ichneumon wasp drills into a tree to sting a wood wasp larva. She then injects an egg into it. When the egg hatches, it will feed on its host.

DID YOU KNOW?
There are at least 20,000 species of wasps, of which 19,000 or so are solitary.

Under Attack

The stingers of bees and wasps offer good protection against predators, but they must still be on their guard. Mice, birds, toads, spiders, and a host of other creatures all eat bees and wasps. If a bee or wasp gets caught in a spider web, the spider will first wrap it in its sticky silk so that it cannot sting, then it will eat it. Several species of wasps hunt other wasps and bees, including the bee wolf, a large wasp that feeds on honey bees. It stings a bee to paralyze it, then drags it back to its burrow.

> DID YOU KNOW?
>
> **The robber fly can accelerate from 0 to 25 miles per hour (40 km/h) in just 2 seconds.**

DAYLIGHT ROBBERY
Robber flies prey on bees and wasps. They snatch them in mid-air, stab them to death with their sharp mouthparts, then suck out their insides.

237

Poison in the Water

Venomous creatures also lurk in the sea—and some are deadly. Fish, jellyfish, octopuses, and shells can cause nasty wounds and even kill with their poisons. Humans are usually affected when they step on camouflaged fish such as the stonefish (below), or try to touch pretty creatures like the lionfish (right).

Hidden Danger

Step on a stonefish and you are in for a nasty shock. The spines on this odd-looking creature contain the most toxic venom of any fish. The pain it causes is intense and without first aid, the victim may die. The stonefish often lies still in shallow waters and, as its name suggests, it looks like a stone on the seafloor. Algae even grow on the fish, just as they do on rocks. That makes it hard to spot, and a hazard for human bathers.

SPOT THE FISH
The stonefish's lumpy shape and patterned skin cause it to merge with the seabed. In certain conditions, it is almost impossible to see.

ANIMAL OR MINERAL?
Stonefish live in the shallow waters of the Red Sea, Indian Ocean, and southwestern Pacific Ocean. They often lurk on coral reefs.

Prize Fighters

With their bright colors and spectacular fins, lionfish are among the most beautiful creatures in the sea and are often displayed in aquariums. But they are also fierce predators and capable of giving swimmers and careless fish collectors a nasty shock. The lionfish's fins conceal sharp spines, which are poisonous and can inflict a painful wound. The lionfish may even attack a potential predator by thrusting its spines forward.

ROUND UP

A red lionfish hunts on a reef in the Philippines. Lionfish use their long fins to trap crabs, shrimps, and small fish, then snap them up with a quick bite.

DID YOU KNOW?

Lionfish and their relatives the scorpionfish sting up to 50,000 people a year.

REEF CREEPER

Lionfish are also known as firefish, turkeyfish, and butterfly cod. They are found mainly on coral reefs of the Indian and Pacific oceans.

Bats of the Sea

Rays are related to sharks. They are also known as batoids, which comes from a Greek word that means "sharks" or "skates." The members of one group of rays, the stingrays, have one or more spines on their long tails, and in most cases the spines are poisonous. When a stingray is threatened or touched, it lashes out with its tail. The spine can make deep wounds that take a long time to heal and can even be fatal, and the poison can make humans quite sick.

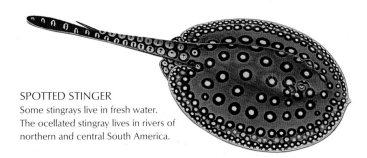

SPOTTED STINGER
Some stingrays live in fresh water. The ocellated stingray lives in rivers of northern and central South America.

GETTING TO THE POINT

The spine on a stingray's tail can measure up to 1 foot (30 cm) long.

ON THE LOOKOUT
The stingray's mouth is on its underside, and its eyes are on the upper edge of its body. This lets it feed on the seafloor while keeping an eye out for predators.

Special Deliveries

Fish deliver venom in a range of ways. Many, such as catfish and zebrafish, have spines on the fins on their backs, which jab venom into predators. Surgeonfish have tiny, poisonous spines on the sides of their tails. When a school of surgeonfish swims past a predator, flicking their tails, they cause numerous cuts that take a long time to heal. Pufferfish release poison into the water when threatened, and are also poisonous to eat.

AIRBAG PROTECTION

When a pufferfish is alarmed, it pumps water into a bag in its stomach. This makes it look bigger and pushes out its venomous spines.

UNDER PRESSURE

If a catfish is touched, three poisonous spines spring out from its body—one on its back and one on each side.

A DEADLY DELICACY
Pufferfish are considered a delicacy in Japan. They must be cut and cooked carefully to avoid poisoning the eater.

DID YOU KNOW?

One tiny drop of poison from a pufferfish is enough to kill a human.

Monsters of the Deep

Squid are among the largest underwater carnivores. Capable of terrific speeds, they race up to large fish and shellfish and grab them with their tentacles. In many squid, the tentacles have sharp hooks and spines tipped with a deadly poison that paralyzes prey. The squid then chews its victim with its horny beak, and swallows it in chunks. Squid attacks on humans have been recorded, but none has caused death or serious injury.

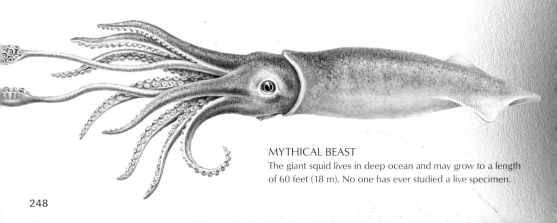

MYTHICAL BEAST
The giant squid lives in deep ocean and may grow to a length of 60 feet (18 m). No one has ever studied a live specimen.

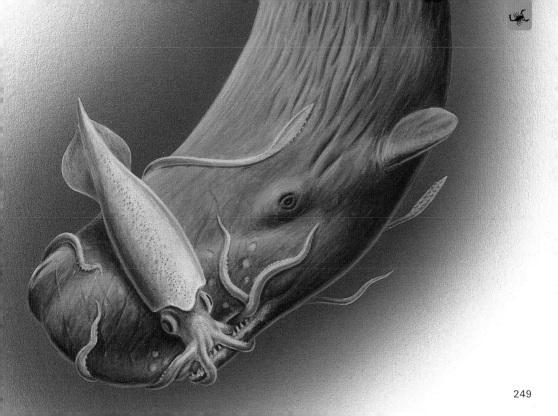

Odd One Out

As well as their eight long, strong arms, octopuses have another powerful weapon: venom. The poison is made by glands in the octopus's mouth. An octopus bites into prey to paralyze it, or, in some cases, spits poison onto its victim. However, in every case except one, the poison is not harmful to humans. The exception is the tiny blue-ringed octopus of Australia, whose bite can kill a person in minutes. And there is no antivenin.

HAZARD LIGHTS
When threatened, the blue rings of the blue-ringed octopus become a much brighter color.

KEEPING THEIR DISTANCE
Some octopuses have effective camouflage that helps them surprise prey and avoid predators. Even large octopuses are fearful of humans and usually keep well away from them.

Mindless Menaces

Jellyfish have no brain, eyes, or heart, yet they are still efficient hunters. Most have a body, called a bell, and long tentacles. These tentacles are armed with stinging cells called nematocysts. Whenever a tentacle comes into contact with another creature, it stings. Small creatures die and are eaten. Large ones beat a hasty retreat.

SHORT-LIVED STINGER

In young jellyfish, the bell develops first, then the tentacles. Most jellyfish live for only a few weeks.

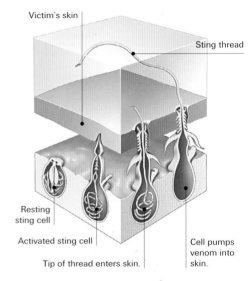

Victim's skin

Sting thread

Resting sting cell

Activated sting cell

Tip of thread enters skin.

Cell pumps venom into skin.

THREAT FROM A THREAD

Each jellyfish tentacle carries millions of stinging cells. When activated, a stinging cell fires a microscopic thread into the victim's body, through which it injects venom.

MOCK JELLYFISH
Though it looks like a jellyfish, the Portuguese man-of-war belongs to a different group, the siphonophores. It can also inflict painful wounds, though they fade fairly quickly.

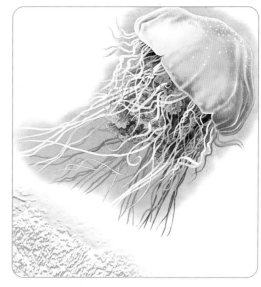

YELLOW GIANT
The bell of a lion's mane jellyfish can grow to a diameter of 8 feet (2.4 m) and its tentacles can reach 100 feet (30 m). It lives in arctic seas and eats plankton, fish, and other jellyfish.

The Box Jellyfish

Jellyfish can inflict severe stings on humans, but only a few can kill. By far the most deadly is the box jellyfish, also known as the sea wasp. Its excruciating stings have killed many people in the coastal tropical waters of the Indian and Pacific oceans. The box jellyfish is a strong swimmer and can sense large objects. Its bell is larger than a man's head, and its tentacles can grow to 10 feet (3 m). Yet, its transparent body makes it extremely difficult to see.

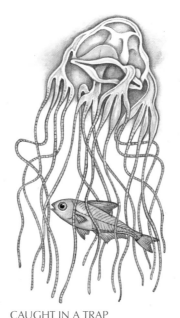

CAUGHT IN A TRAP
As well as poison, the box jellyfish's tentacles carry small hooks and sticky liquid that help trap prey.

DID YOU KNOW?

A single adult box jellyfish carries enough venom to kill about 60 people.

LASTING EFFECTS
The stinging tentacles of the box jellyfish not only poison their victim but leave long scars on the skin. These may take many months to heal.

Pretty and Poisonous

Some of the prettiest sights in the sea are among the most dangerous. Beautiful cone shells shoot out harpoon-like spines attached to small tubes that pump poison into their victims. Sea anemones wave colorful but highly venomous tentacles. The blue sea slug collects stinging cells from jellyfish and uses them to defend itself. Fire coral causes burning or stinging rashes on the skin of any creature unfortunate enough to brush against it.

AN UNFRIENDLY WAVE

Stings from some sea anemones can cause pain, burns, and fever.

STRANGE FRUIT

Stings from sea urchin spines are painful and can damage flesh.

DEADLY EFFECTS
The tulip cone is one of the most dangerous cone shells. Cone shell venom can cause pain, paralysis, and heart and lung failure.

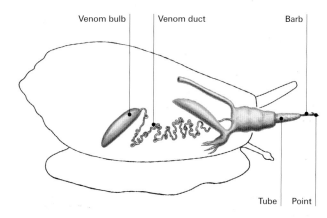

Venom bulb | Venom duct | Barb

Tube | Point

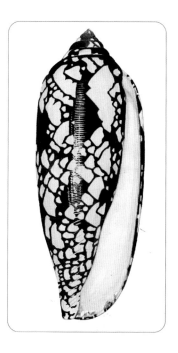

COMING OUT OF ITS SHELL
Inside the pretty exterior of a cone shell, like this aulicus cone, is a lethal weapon. The darts fired by cone shells can be 0.4 inch (1 cm) long.

DID YOU KNOW?
Three species of cone shell, including the tulip cone, are able to kill humans.

NATURAL WEAPONS

Kick Boxers

If you had to defend yourself, you would kick with your feet as well as hit with your hands. Many animals do the same, and some kick harder than others. Among the hardest kickers are some of the ungulates—animals with hooves. Horses and deer, for example, have thick, hard, sharp-edged hooves that can stun or even kill another animal. Horses and their relatives tend to kick with their rear feet. Deer also use their front feet to fight rivals.

FLYING HOOVES
To defend themselves from predators, such as African hunting dogs, zebras kick out fiercely with one or both of their powerful back legs.

Toes and Spurs

As well as heavy feet, some animals have sharp toes or spurs that can cause nasty wounds. Among them are several large, flightless birds. Although they are unable to fly, these birds can run fast and will always try to flee danger first. But, if cornered, they will kick hard and fast. The male jungle fowl, for example, has razor-edged spurs. The cassowary has one long, dagger-like claw on each foot, which it uses to stab and slash attackers.

BIG KICKER

Cassowaries are large birds that live in Australia and New Guinea.

THE SHARP END

The claw on the cassowary's inner toe may be 5 inches (12 cm) long.

PROTECTIVE PARENT
The emu, which lives in Australia, is generally not aggressive. But if an animal or person comes between an emu and its young, it will kick and scratch fiercely to defend its chicks.

Handle with Care

Vibrant colors are often a warning sign that an animal has another trick up its sleeve—poison. Some brightly colored creatures produce chemicals that can harm predators that try to eat or even just touch them. Many caterpillars and butterflies, for example, carry toxins that burn. Several jungle-dwelling frogs and some newts and salamanders have deadly poison in their skin. There is even one species of bird, the pitohui, that has poison on its feathers.

A WINNING TIP

The Chocó Indians of South America make their arrow tips more effective by rubbing them on poison frogs. The poison kills the animal much more quickly than the arrow alone.

DID YOU KNOW?

An adult rough-skinned newt has enough poison in its skin to kill ten adult humans.

PINT-SIZED POISONER

Poison frogs live in tropical forests in South America. They are tiny, but the poison on their skin is among the most toxic substances found on Earth.

Toxic Toads

Predators cannot rely on color to warn them about poison, because many dull-colored animals also pack a poisonous punch. For example, almost all toads can squeeze a gooey, toxic substance out of their skin. When a predator bites, it · immediately tastes something foul and lets go of the toad. In some cases, the poison can make the predator sick or even kill it. However, toad poisons are not harmful to humans—unless you, too, try to eat a toad!

NASTY SURPRISE
Cane toads have spread to places where they did not formerly live. In these areas, predators often die when they try to eat the unfamiliar toads.

UNFRIENDLY FOAM
Like many toads, the cane, or marine, toad squeezes foam out of glands on its back. Cane toad venom can kill a dog.

Power Points

You may not think you could defend yourself with your hair. But a few mammals do just that. Porcupines and echidnas have developed hard, pointed hairs called quills, which grow all over their bodies. This spiky coat provides strong protection against predators. The crested porcupine, which lives in southern Europe and Africa, even charges backward to spear its foes. It has been known to kill hyenas, lions, and humans.

DIGGING TO SAFETY
Found in Australia and New Guinea, echidnas uses their long, sticky tongues to pick up termites. When threatened, they dig into the ground so that only their quills are visible.

BRISTLING WITH SPEARS

A crested porcupine's quills may be up to 14 inches (36 cm) long.

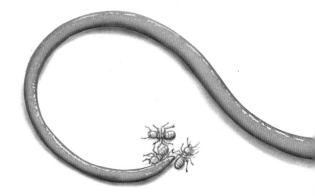

When Bigger Is Better

Size makes a big difference in the animal kingdom. A small cat looks like a pet, but a big cat is a terrifying predator. A little lizard poses no threat, but a large one can be a fierce and dangerous enemy. Many big creatures, such as whales, elephants, and bears, can rely on their size to deter would-be attackers and, as a result, have few predators. They may not be aggressive themselves, but they can still hurt people or cause serious damage with their big bodies.

ENTER THE DRAGON
The komodo dragon of Indonesia is the biggest lizard in the world. It has sharp claws and teeth, and can move surprisingly quickly. It preys on animals up to three times its weight.

DID YOU KNOW?

Large whales sometimes sink boats accidentally by surfacing underneath them.

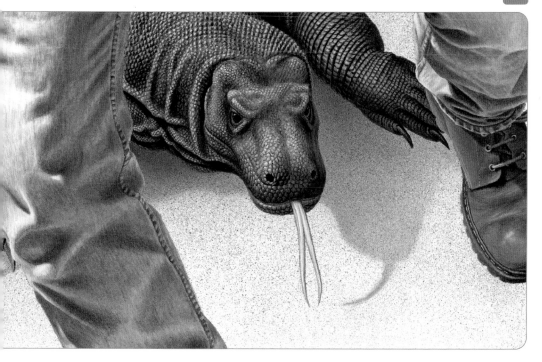

Shock Tactics

Some water-dwellers stun prey and scare off attackers by giving them an electric shock. Electric rays have organs behind their eyes that make currents of up to 200 volts, which would give you a nasty jolt. The African electric catfish can produce up to 400 volts. That's topped by the electric eel, which can generate 550 volts—enough to knock you over.

POWER OUTLETS

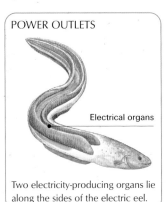

Electrical organs

Two electricity-producing organs lie along the sides of the electric eel.

RAPID RESPONSE

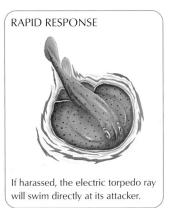

If harassed, the electric torpedo ray will swim directly at its attacker.

DID YOU KNOW?

The ancient Greeks and Romans used electric rays to treat headaches.

273

Quick off the Mark

A sudden burst of acceleration can quickly turn the tables on a predator or prey. So it is not surprising that many animals rely on speed as their most effective weapon. Over a short distance, no land animal can outrun a cheetah, so as long as this cat can get close enough to its target it is almost guaranteed a meal. Similarly, a peregrine falcon's tremendous speed allows it to fall quickly on unsuspecting prey.

FASTEST OF ALL
The peregrine falcon lives in many environments, even cities. It is not only the fastest bird, but the fastest animal of all. It can dive at speeds of up to 200 miles per hour (320 km/h).

FASTEST HUMAN

The fastest speed run by a human is about 22 miles per hour (37 km/h).

ANCIENT ATHLETE

Struthiomimus, the fastest dinosaur, ran at 40 miles per hour (64 km/h).

LAND CHAMP

A cheetah can quickly reach 70 miles per hour (110 km/h).

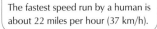

Survival of the Strongest

When an animal lacks weapons such as tusks or poison, its survival may depend on simple physical strength. The size of a bear or gorilla lets it overpower rivals. But small animals can also be surprisingly powerful. The wolverine, for example, is only as large as a medium-sized dog, but strong enough to kill a moose. A tiny rhinoceros beetle can lift 850 times its own weight.

STRENGTH IN RESERVE
A large gorilla is hugely powerful and could easily kill a human. But gorillas are vegetarians and use their strength only for defense and foraging for food.

Mass Attacks

When they band together in large groups, some relatively harmless animals can become dangerous, while other already dangerous animals become even more deadly. The sting from a single bee or wasp, for example, might not do much harm. But if an entire swarm attacks, it can kill an animal—even a human. By working together in packs, animals such as wolves and hyenas can capture creatures much bigger than themselves.

MULTIPLE KILLERS
Large swarms of African bees can kill animals and people. These bees were introduced to South America in 1957 and have since spread north.

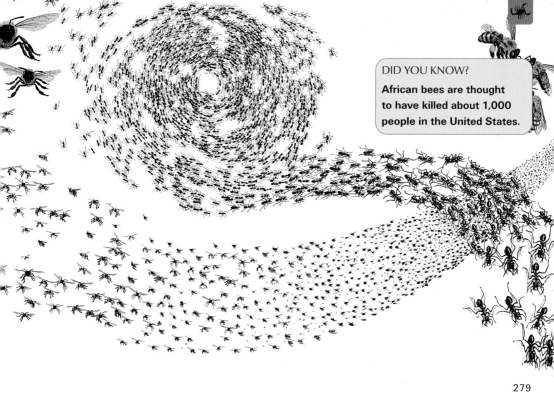

On the March

Ants work together to build their nests, breed, and, in some cases, kill. An ant colony can include anything from a few dozen to 300 million ants. Many ants are carnivores and they often go on the march in huge groups in search of food. In Africa, swarms of up to 20 million driver ants advance across a wide area, killing with bites and stings, then eating, any unfortunate animals that are caught in their path.

OVERWHELMING FORCE
These ants have swarmed all over a hornet. Some hold its legs, while others bite and sting its body. Eventually, the hornet will die and the ants will feast on it.

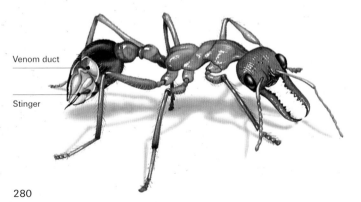

Venom duct

Stinger

BITE OF THE BULLDOG
Australia's bulldog ant uses its massive jaws to grab prey, then poisons it with its venomous stinger. Bulldog ants often attack in groups. As few as 30 stings from these ants can kill a human.

Disease Carriers

Among the deadliest animals are insects that carry diseases. For example, some mosquitoes carry a bug called *Plasmodium*. When people are bitten by these mosquitoes, they develop a disease called malaria, which is frequently fatal.

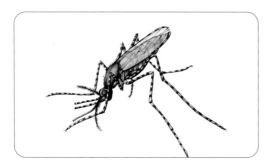

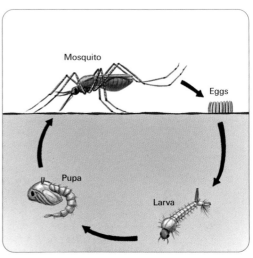

PUBLIC ENEMY
Mosquitoes carry the malaria bug in their salivary glands. Malaria may have caused half of all human deaths since the Stone Age. It still kills about 2 million people every year.

BIRTH OF A TINY KILLER
Mosquitoes lay their eggs in water. The eggs become larvae, which feed on tiny plants and animals. The larvae then become pupae, which turn into adult mosquitoes.

BLOOD SUCKER

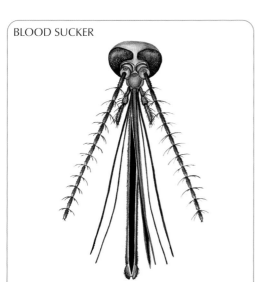

This close-up view of a mosquito's head shows its long, hollow proboscis. The mosquito inserts the proboscis into an animal, then sucks up its blood.

SPREADING SLEEP

The tsetse fly drinks the blood of humans and cattle, feeding until its belly is swollen. It often passes on a disease called sleeping sickness, which can kill people.

Pests and Plagues

Insects are not the only animals that carry diseases. Some mammals transmit dangerous illnesses when they bite or scratch, or carry small insects that can infect people. Some of the worst diseases in history, called plagues, were passed from person to person by fleas living in the fur of rats. Plagues have killed millions of people. It was not until the early twentieth century that effective treatments were developed.

RABID RACCOONS

Small numbers of raccoons carry rabies, a very dangerous disease.

STILL A THREAT

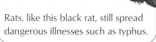

Rats, like this black rat, still spread dangerous illnesses such as typhus.

STEER CLEAR

Squirrels can carry rabies but seldom infect humans.

EXTENDED FAMILY

Brown rats live in groups of up to 200. They eat almost anything and will attack rabbits and other small animals.

DID YOU KNOW?

Between 1346 and 1350 one-third of the people in Europe died of a plague.

Playing Host

Wherever you are and whatever you are doing, you are no doubt surrounded by, and perhaps even carrying, parasites. Parasites are tiny creatures that feed on other animals. They can be dangerous because they may hurt their host or pass on serious diseases. However, many, such as mites that feed on dust and skin, are so small that we cannot see them and barely notice their effects.

BLOOD THIRSTY
Ticks cling to animals and drink their blood. They pierce the skin and vein with needle-like mouthparts, then suck up the blood until full.

DID YOU KNOW?

The largest tapeworms found inside humans have measured 60 feet (18 m) long.

GUT INSTINCT

Tapeworms are found in some foods. When eaten, they take up residence in the animal's intestines and stomach, where they absorb digested food.

The Most Dangerous Animal

Did you know that you are a member of the most dangerous species of all? No animal has caused more harm to other creatures or the environment than humans. For thousands of years, people have killed animals for their meat, skins, and other materials. Humans have spread over the globe, and in many cases, destroyed the habitats of other creatures. As a result, some plants and animals have declined in number or even disappeared.

IN OUR SIGHTS
Humans even kill animals they don't eat. Rhinos, for example, are hunted only for their horns, which are kept as trophies or used to make medicines.

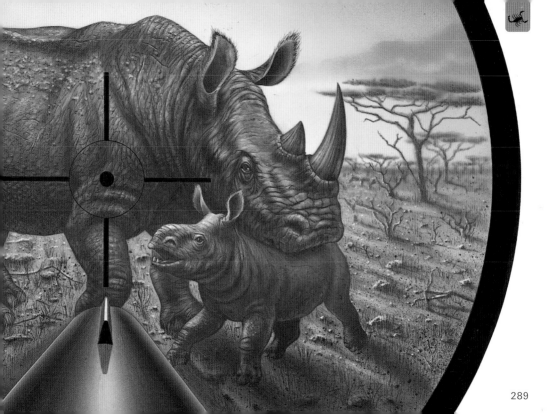

Hunting to Excess

In modern times, human hunting has affected animals much more than it did in earlier centuries. That is because humans now have powerful weapons, traps, and poisons that can kill many more animals and destroy more of the places where they live. Bulldozers and chainsaws allow people to clear forests rapidly so that they can build houses. At sea, large ships carrying giant nets can haul in thousands of fish at a time.

CARVINGS

Humans use carved and painted whale teeth as ornaments.

HUNTED TO THE BRINK
In the nineteenth and twentieth centuries, humans killed enormous numbers of whales. As a result, many whale species are now rare.

Accidental Damage

Humans not only hunt animals deliberately, they also harm them accidentally and at times without realizing. When people catch large numbers of fish, many ocean predators, such as sharks and dolphins, are left with little food, making it harder for them to survive. Large structures built by humans, such as oil pipelines, roads, and tall buildings can stop animals reaching mates and can even kill migrating birds.

DID YOU KNOW?

For every human killed by sharks, two million sharks are killed by humans.

HOPELESSLY ENTANGLED

Modern fishing nets that are meant for catching small fish often trap larger sea creatures. Hammerhead sharks are among the species that suffer.

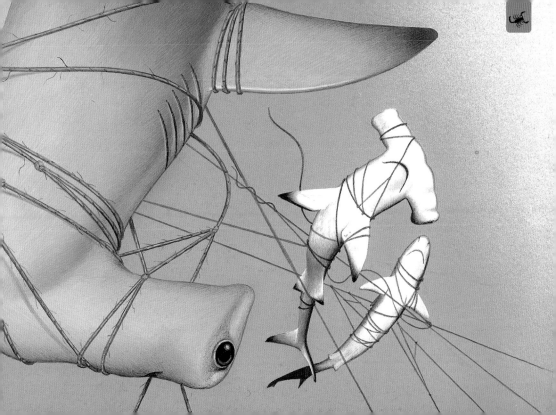

Trail of Destruction

Humans have left a trail of destruction around the globe. They have wiped out plants and animals, cut down forests, and poisoned rivers and seas with toxic chemicals. By clearing land in dry areas, they have caused deserts to spread. Their factories and cars have filled the air with toxic gases. Some of these gases make rain more acidic, which in turn kills plants.

GLOBAL DAMAGE
This map shows the various ways in which humans have damaged the environment, and the places where the damage is greatest.

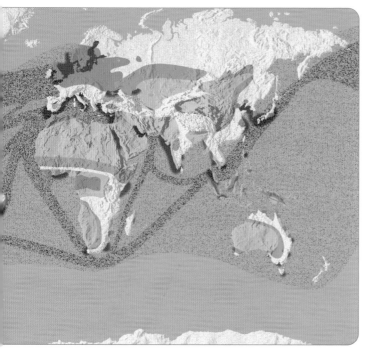

 Remaining rain forest

 Original rain forest

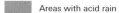 Areas with acid rain

 Polluted waterways

Light oil slicks from shipping

 Heavy oil slicks from shipping

Deserts

Areas at risk of
becoming desert

Forced From Their Homes

As the human population has grown, so has our need for land. All over the world, people have cut down forests and cleared grasslands to make room for towns and farms, and to obtain building materials and fuel. In doing this, they have destroyed the homes and food supplies of plants and animals. Although some creatures can find new places to live, others cannot and quickly die out.

CUT TO THE GROUND
Rain forests are home to about half of all the plant and animal species on Earth. Humans have already cut down more than half of these forests.

The Perils of Pollution

Humans dump waste on land and into seas and rivers, and pollute the air with smoke from factories and cars. As a result, animals suffer and die. Poisons released into rivers kill fish and spread disease. Chemicals sprayed onto crops make birds sick. Animals also die as a result of choking on things like discarded plastic bags, and are hurt by broken bottles and soft-drink cans.

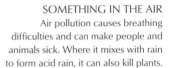

SOMETHING IN THE AIR
Air pollution causes breathing difficulties and can make people and animals sick. Where it mixes with rain to form acid rain, it can also kill plants.

HOW OIL SPOILS
Oil spilled into the sea by tankers can devastate wildlife. With its fur covered in oil, this sea otter can no longer keep dry and warm. Without help, it may die from the cold.

Animals in Danger

As a result of human activities such as hunting, land clearance, and dumping of waste, thousands of plant and animal species have already become extinct and many more are endangered. The rate of extinction has increased rapidly in recent years. In response, many governments and individuals have formed conservation groups to try to protect remaining wildlife.

RARE BREED
Golden lion tamarins live in Brazil, where they have been hunted for their skins. Today, only about 800 remain in the wild.

DID YOU KNOW?

At least 50 species become extinct every day, mainly as a result of human activities.

WIPED OUT
Humans first came across the dodo, a large flightless bird, in 1507. By 1680, they had hunted them to extinction.

FACING EXTINCTION

Without protection, orangutans may become extinct within ten years.

Where in the World?

 African bee

 African elephant

 American alligator

 Anaconda

 Army ant

 Asian elephant

 Barracuda

 Black-headed sea snake

 Black rat

 Black widow spider

 Blue-ringed octopus

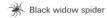 Box jellyfish

 Brown bear

 Bulldog ant

 Desert locust

 Estuarine crocodile

 European wasp

 Funnel-web spider

Gaur

Grizzly bear

Hippopotamus

King cobra

Lesser weeverfish

Lion

Nile crocodile

North African scorpion

Poison frog

Portuguese man-of-war

 Scorpion

Spitting cobra

Stonefish

Tiger

Wandering spider

Western diamond rattlesnake

White rhino

DANGER EVERYWHERE

Dangerous creatures lurk in almost every corner of the globe. Most regions have at least one predator that is larger than humans. But we are more likely to be struck by lightning than attacked by any of these creatures.

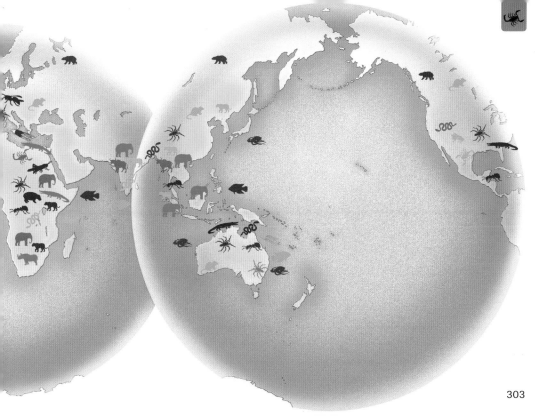

Glossary

acid rain Rain that has combined with air pollution to form an acid. Acid rain can kill trees and other plants, and damage buildings.

adaptation A feature of an animal or plant that helps it survive in a particular environment.

antenna An organ on an animal's head that it uses to sense its surroundings. Insects usually have two antennae.

antivenin A medicine given to someone who has been bitten or stung by a venomous creature, to stop them getting sick.

antlers Bony growths that sprout on the heads of deer and moose. In most cases, antlers fall off once a year then regrow.

aquatic Living in water all or most of the time.

bell The soft, dome-shaped part of a jellyfish. On most jellyfish, tentacles hang below the bell.

bird of prey A bird that hunts and kills animals, including other birds.

camouflage Colors and patterns on an animal that enable it to blend in with its surroundings.

canine teeth The teeth, often pointed, at the front sides of an animal's mouth, between the incisors and molars.

carcass The body of an animal that has been killed.

carnivore An animal that eats mainly meat.

carrion The rotting flesh and other remains of dead animals.

claw A sharp, usually curved nail on the end of an animal's toes.

colony A large number of animals that live, hunt, and defend themselves together.

conservation The protection of Earth's resources.

crocodilian A member of the group of animals that is made up of crocodiles, alligators, caimans, and gharials.

drone A male bee whose sole role is to mate with the queen.

echolocation A system of navigation that relies on sound to detect objects. Dolphins, porpoises, bats, and some birds use echolocation when hunting.

endangered species An animal that is likely to become extinct unless humans take action to protect it.

evolution The gradual changes that take place in animals and plants to help them operate efficiently in a particular environment.

extinct No longer alive. When the last living member of a species dies, the species is said to be extinct.

fang A long tooth. Fangs are often hollow and used to inject venom.

fossil The remains or imprint of an animal or plant in rock. Fossils tell us what prehistoric and other extinct animals looked like.

gills Organs that extract oxygen from water. Animals with gills include fish and tadpoles.

habitat The area in which an animal normally lives.

hatchling A baby animal that has just emerged from an egg.

herbivore An animal that eats mainly plants.

hoof The thick, hard casing that covers the toes of horses, deer, and related animals.

horn A bony growth that sprouts on the head of some animals, such as wild cattle, antelopes, and rhinos. Unlike antlers, horns are usually permanent.

host An animal or plant on which a parasite feeds.

incisor teeth The front teeth of an animal, which are normally used for tearing food.

invertebrate An animal with no backbone. Invertebrates include insects, spiders, jellyfish, octopuses, and cone shells.

keratin The material of which hair, fingernails and horns are made.

larva An insect in the first stage of its life after coming out of the egg.

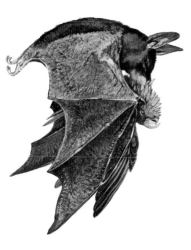

mammal A warm-blooded animal that has a backbone and feeds its young with milk. Most mammals also give birth to live young and have hairy bodies.

migration A journey taken by an animal, usually in summer and winter, to move between breeding and feeding grounds.

mites A group of tiny eight-legged, insect-like animals that are related to ticks. Many are parasites.

molars The side and back teeth of a mammal, normally used for crushing and grinding.

nocturnal Active at night. Animals that are nocturnal usually sleep during the day.

organ A part of the body with a particular function. The heart, brain, and liver are all organs.

paralyze To prevent an animal's body working. Many animals use venom to paralyze prey, so that it cannot run away.

parasite A plant or animal that lives or feeds on another plant or animal.

pedipalps A pair of leglike organs on the head of some insects, spiders, and scorpions, which are used for feeling or handling food. Spiders also use their pedipalps during mating.

pinniped A carnivorous marine mammal with four flippers. Pinnipeds spend much of their time in the sea but must return to land to breed. They include seals, sea lions, and walruses.

plankton Tiny organisms that float in the sea. Some are plants and some are animals.

poison A substance that causes illness or death when touched or eaten, even in small amounts.

predator An animal that hunts, kills, and eats other animals. Its victims are called prey.

prey An animal that is hunted, killed, and eaten by other animals. Its attackers are called predators.

proboscis In insects, a long mouthpart or tongue used for feeding. In mammals, a long nose, snout, or trunk.

queen A female insect that starts a colony. The queen is normally the only female to lay eggs.

quill A long, sharp hair used for defense. Animals with quills include porcupines and echidnas.

rack A pair of antlers.

rain forest Tropical forest that receives at least 100 inches (250 cm) of rain each year. Rain forests are home to a vast number of plant and animal species.

reptile An animal with a backbone and dry, scaly skin. Reptiles include snakes, lizards, turtles, crocodiles, and alligators.

retractable claws Claws that can be drawn back inside the skin or fur to protect them when not in use. Most cats have retractable claws.

rodent A small mammal, usually with short legs and two pairs of large incisor teeth, which it uses to gnaw through tough foods such as seeds and nuts. Rodents include mice, rats, and squirrels.

scavenger An animal that feeds on dead animals, often the remains of animals killed by predators.

social insect An insect that lives in a colony with other insects of the same species. Social insects include many kinds of bees and wasps.

solitary Living alone rather than in a group or colony.

species A group of animals that look the same and are able to breed together and produce fertile young.

spinnerets Finger-like organs on the rear end of a spider, which are connected to its silk glands and used to spin the silk threads the spider uses to make webs.

spur A sharp, pointed nail on the leg of a bird or platypus.

stinger A hard, hollow, point on the tail or head of an insect that is used to inject venom.

talon A claw, usually found on a bird of prey.

tentacle A long, thin, flexible body part on a sea creature, which is used to feel, grasp, and sometimes sting.

territory An area of land used by an animal and guarded against intruders. It usually contains everything the animal needs, including food, water, and a place to sleep or nest.

toxin A poisonous substance. Venoms are made up of toxins.

tusk A very long tooth often used in fights and for defense. Animals with tusks include elephants, walruses, and narwhals.

ungulate A large, plant-eating animal with hooves. Ungulates include deer, antelopes, cattle, elephants, and rhinoceroses.

venom Poison injected into prey by animals, often through a stinger, fangs, spines, or tentacles.

venom gland The part of an animal's body that makes its venom.

venom sac The place in an animal's body where venom is stored until it is needed.

venomous Capable of poisoning prey with venom.

vertebrate An animal with a backbone. Vertebrates include mammals, fish, reptiles, amphibians, and birds.

worker A social insect that collects food and raises young but does not usually reproduce.

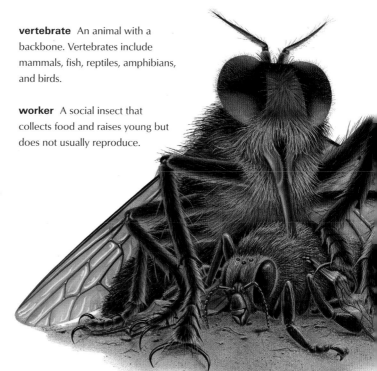

Index

Acknowledgments

PHOTOGRAPHIC CREDITS

Key t=top; l=left; r=right; tl=top left; tcl=top center left; tc=top center; tcr=top center right; tr=top right; cl=center left; c=center; cr=center right; b=bottom; bl=bottom left; bcl=bottom center left; bc=bottom center; bcr=bottom center right; br=bottom right

AUS = Auscape International; COR = Corel Corp.; DS = Digital Stock; DV = Digital Vision; iS = istockphoto.com; PD = Photodisc; PL = photolibrary.com; WA = Wildlife Art Ltd

13c COR **20**bc iS **27**c PD **28**bc COR **29**c DS **30**bl iS **31**c PL **33**c PD **36**bl iS **43**c PD **62**bl iS **67**c iS **85**c iS **91**c PD **116**bl COR **141**l iS **149**c COR **205**c DV **241**c DS **242**bl COR **243**c iS **245**c iS **246**bl iS **247**r COR **250**c iS **254**c AUS **264**bl iS **267**c iS **273**c PL **281**c iS **287**c iS **298**bl PD **299**c iS **301**c COR **307**br iS

ILLUSTRATION CREDITS

Alan Ewart, Alistair Barnard, Anne Bowman, Barbara Rodanska, Bernard Tate, Peter Bull Art Studio, Chris Forsey, Chris Shields/The Art Agency, Chris Turnbull/The Art Agency, Christer Eriksson, Claudia Saraceni, David Kirshner, Frank Knight, Genevieve Wallace, Gino Hasler, Giuliano Fornari, Guy Troughton, Glen Vause, Ian Jackson/The Art Agency, James McKinnon, Jane Beatson, John Francis/Bernard Thornton Artists UK, John Mac/FOLIO, John Richards, Jon Gittoes, Kevin Stead, Luis Rey/The Art Agency, MG = Illustrations © MagicGroup

s.r.o. (Czech Republic) www.magicgroup.cz, Marjorie Crosby-Fairall, Mark Dando/The Art Agency, Mark Iley/The Art Agency, Martin Camm, Mike Atkinson/Garden Studio, Mike Gorman, Peter Schouten, Peter Scott/The Art Agency, Priscilla Barret/The Art Agency, Ray Grinaway, Richard McKennar, Rob Mancini, Robert Hynes, Roger Swainston, Sally Beech, Sandra Doyle/The Art Agency, Simone End, Steve White/The Art Agency, Stuart McVicar, Susanna Addario, Tim Hayward/Bernard Thornton Artists UK, Tony Pyrzakowski, Trevor Ruth

INDEX

Puddingburn Publishing Services

CONSULTANT

Dr George McKay has studied mammals and birds around the world. His scientific work has ranged from the ecology of Asiatic elephants to the taxonomy of Australian marsupials. He recently retired from Sydney's Macquarie University where he is now an Honorary Associate. He has been consultant editor on a number of books including Weldon Owen's *Encyclopedia of Animals* and *Children's Encyclopedia of Animals*.